SEX TRAFFICKING

SEX TRAFFICKING
A Global Perspective

Edited by
Kimberly A. McCabe
and
Sabita Manian

LEXINGTON BOOKS
A division of
ROWMAN & LITTLEFIELD PUBLISHERS, INC.
Lanham • Boulder • New York • Toronto • Plymouth, UK

Published by Lexington Books
A division of Rowman & Littlefield Publishers, Inc.
A wholly owned subsidiary of The Rowman & Littlefield Publishing Group, Inc.
4501 Forbes Boulevard, Suite 200, Lanham, Maryland 20706
http://www.lexingtonbooks.com

Estover Road, Plymouth PL6 7PY, United Kingdom

Copyright © 2010 by Lexington Books

British Library Cataloguing in Publication Information Available

Library of Congress Cataloging-in-Publication Data

Sex trafficking : a global perspective / edited by Kimberly A. McCabe and Sabita Manian.
    p. cm.
  Includes bibliographical references and index.
  ISBN 978-0-7391-2933-3 (cloth : alk. paper) — ISBN 978-0-7391-2934-0 (pbk. : alk.
paper) — ISBN 978-0-7391-4728-3 (electronic)
  1. Human trafficking. 2. Prostitution. I. McCabe, Kimberly A., 1965– II. Manian, Sabita.
  HQ281.S487 2010
  364.15'3—dc22
                                    2010000719

Printed in the United States of America

Contents

1

Introduction:
Defining Sex Trafficking

Kimberly A. McCabe and Sabita Manian

FROM LONDON TO LUSAKA, FROM MUMBAI to Mombasa, the common thread of heinous crime that afflicts thousands of women, children, men and thence the fabric of human society is the malaise of human sex trafficking. Whether it is the realm of sports or tourism, conflict or calamity, a familiar predicament for many countries is organized criminal networks that mobilize into action by preying on human victims and the flesh trade even as they (the criminal enterprises) churn out global profits amounting to billions of dollars. For instance, not only did incidence of sex trafficking double during the Olympic Games in Athens but as London prepares for hosting its Olympic games in 2012 an increase in the number of trafficked women working in the five Olympic host boroughs has already been noted (BBC News, 2009). Similar trends are more predictable, however, in violent, non-peacetime situations when the "by-products of armed conflict—poverty and joblessness—can create extremely perilous conditions for young girls, including trafficking for sexual exploitation" (UNICEF 2009, 33).

The profits generated from this nefarious crime by humans against other humans, according to one estimate, has increased from what used to be a US$12 billion enterprise to a US$36 billion venture (IOM, 2009). Global estimates of human trafficking range from four million to 600,000 victims each year (IOM)—the majority of those individuals are victims of *sex* trafficking—revealing the difficulty in data gathering and accountability. Currently, the U.S. State Department estimates suggest that approximately 70 percent of the victims of sex trafficking are female and approximately 50 percent of the victims are under the age of 18. Individuals are generally trafficked for one of two main reasons: labor or sex. However, these researchers acknowledge that individuals may also be trafficking for adoption, soldiering, camel jockeying, marriage, and organs. Victims of sex trafficking may be forced into prostitution, pornography, prostitution for the military or militia, spousal prostitution, and prostitution for the sex-tourism industry.

Many nations have either misunderstood the definition of human trafficking or failed to comprehend the magnitude of incidents of trafficking that have occurred within their own geographical borders, or have simply lacked the wherewithal to combat human sex trafficking. The United Nations has defined *human trafficking* as the recruitment, transfer, harboring or receipt of persons by threat or use of force. This definition is similar to that used by the U.S. State Department's Trafficking Victims Protection Act of 2000 (henceforth TVPA) which describes severe forms of trafficking as: (a) sex trafficking in which a commercial sex act is induced by force, fraud, or coercion, or in which the person induced to perform such an act has not attained 18 years of age; or (b) the recruitment, harboring, transportation, provision, or obtaining of a person for labor or services, through the use of force, fraud, or coercion for the purpose of subjection to involuntary servitude, peonage, debt bondage, or slavery (U.S. Department of State, 2008).

Unfortunately, the trafficking of persons, although different from smuggling, is often identified as "people smuggling" (McCabe, 2008). People smuggling is also a global problem as it has quickly become one of the preferred trades for criminal networks (IOM, 1999). However, trafficking is a distinct activity, as the trafficking of persons involves exploitation. Smuggling simply implies enabling the entry into a region of which that person is not a permanent resident (Interpol, 2004). With smuggling, the movement of the individual is always transnational. Human trafficking may occur within the same country. With smuggling, coercion is not an element; those individuals smuggled have freedom of movement and to change employment. This is not the case in human trafficking. Human trafficking is not smuggling; however, the reality of some smuggling cases provides support for their being considered human trafficking cases. Today, as recognized by the United Nations' Definition of Trafficking Protocol, consent to leave one country and work in another country does not distinguish the line between smuggling and human trafficking. If the initial consent of the victim to leave one country for another was gained through deception or coercion, then consent is irrelevant and human trafficking has occurred (McCabe).

For further clarity, in most cases of smuggling, once individuals reach their geographic destination, their relationship with their smuggler is terminated. This is not the case with human trafficking. However, as both involve movement of individuals across borders, they are often confused by governmental officials. This distinction between smuggling and trafficking is important not because of the different dynamics in the criminal activities but also because persons who have been smuggled are not eligible for services that may be provided to victims of human trafficking.

In 2000, with nearly 700,000 individuals trafficked annually, the majority of whom are women and children, the United States Congress passed the *Victims of Trafficking and Violence Protection Act of 2000, P.L. 106–386*, also known as the *Trafficking Victims Protection Act* (TVPA). The TVPA mandated that the U.S. Secretary of State submit a report on "severe forms of trafficking in persons" to Congress, by June 1 (Trafficking in Persons Report, 2001); following this mandate, the State Department has continued to produce an annual report since 2001. The report first identifies if a country is a source (or country of origin) for trafficked victims, a transit, and/or destination country; following this description, the extent of the problem and the degree to which the problem is tackled by the said government leads to the country's ranking in a tier system devised by the State Department. Those countries that fully abide by the TVPA's minimum standards for "elimination of trafficking" are placed on Tier 1. While Tier 1 nations are fully compliant; Tier 2 nations and those on the Tier 2 Watch List do not fully comply, but are making efforts to do so; Tier 3 nations are not compliant and make no significant efforts to do so (TPA, 2001).

When the U.S. Congress passed the TVPA in October 2000, they made an attempt to provide a comprehensive definition of trafficking and to address the issues relating to human trafficking on the national and international levels. After the 2000 TVPA, as cases of human trafficking in the United States and abroad became more prevalent, more legislation was enacted by the Clinton administration. In 2003 President George W. Bush signed the amended *Trafficking Victims Protection Reauthorization Act* (TVPRA), which further strengthened the U.S. government's response to human trafficking by recognizing the needs of the victims of human trafficking. In 2005, the TVPRA was reinforced with proclamations of the United States' support to end this activity and a new phrase, "severe forms of trafficking," was adopted. Thus, the category of *severe forms of trafficking* is expected to include the recruitment, harboring, and so on of a person under one of the following three conditions: (1) human trafficking for labor, (2) human trafficking for commercial sex acts, and (3) human trafficking of those under the age of 18. It is also important to note that through this change in legislation a child under the age of 18 (regardless of country of origin) cannot give his or her consent to be moved from one country to another; thus, a specific type of human trafficking—child trafficking—is identified. In addition, the parent or guardian of the child cannot give consent to the trafficker of that child for his or her movement for the purposes of forced labor or sexual exploitation (UNODC, 2006).

In addition, as clarified in the TVPRA, human trafficking does not require that a victim cross an international border or that the victim be identified as an illegal alien. In July 2004, the Secretary of State, the Secretary of Homeland Security, and the Attorney General created the Human Smuggling and Trafficking Center to serve as a fusion center for information (national and international) on smuggling and trafficking activities. In terms of historical legislation, human trafficking is clearly a human rights violation; however, its effect goes beyond individual outcomes and criminal activity since human trafficking promotes the breakdown of social systems, fuels organized crime, and deprives countries of their most precious resource—human capital. Hence, human sex trafficking is an act that has global consequences.

This book explores the variants of human sex trafficking for Commercial Sexual Exploitation (CSE) from a global perspective in terms of its multiple purposes and its victims. The attempt by the contributors to this volume is to provide (a) a comprehensive scholarly examination and coverage of human sex trafficking (including its prevalence and possibility); and (b) the legal and legislative responses to human trafficking by countries across various geographic regions of the world. The approach is multidisciplinary with scholars from the fields of law, sociology, criminology, history and political science presenting their analyses through the lenses of their respective disciplines. Our introduction presents an overview of the scope of sex trafficking of women and children for commercial sexual exploitation, including the background to the concentrated effort in the United States and particularly the U.S. State Department, which has led to "tier ranking" of countries based on their efforts in preventing human sex trafficking. The subsequent chapters provide an assessment of human sex trafficking in geographical regions as categorized by the U.S. State Department's Annual Report on Trafficking in Persons 2008.

First, we begin our geographical coverage with the region of Africa which includes the subregions of the northern region of the Horn of Africa in the north Southern Africa. The chapter on human sex trafficking in the Horn of Africa by Sabita Manian focuses specially on Somalia with some attention to Ethiopia, Djibouti and Kenya. William Mathias and Kimberly McCabe in their chapter on Southern Africa pay particular attention to South Africa, Mozambique and Zimbabwe. Manian presents Somalia as the classic case of a "failed state" wrestling with countless warring factions including Islamism that has perpetrated large-scale migration and a population vulnerable for exploitation for CSE purposes. In addition to the gender inequality the Horn presents an instance where the absence of state authorities itself is a problem in measuring the scale of the problem of trafficking, along with regional politics that add to the violence and danger for the civilian populations there. Mathias and McCabe's focus on the three southern African states of South Africa, Zimbabwe and Mozambique reveal that migration is a common trend due to political and economic instability (Zimbabwe) and economic volatility (as in the cases of South Africa and Mozambique) leading to the trafficking of their women and children. More particularly, the disempowerment of women and the practices of Lobolo and Kupita Kufa along with the prevailing myths about HIV-AIDS compound the problem and the consequences of trafficking for CSE.

Trafficking in the region of East Asia and the Pacific is highlighted by Yingyu Chen who focuses on Taiwan (Republic of China) and identifies the intraregional or intra-Asian dimension that is peculiar to human sex trafficking in that country and the region and its effects on women migrant workers. Chen shows that women who get exploited in trafficking by entering Taiwan through marriage or tourist visas are much more vulnerable since they do not have recourse to legal help than those who come in through a work visa. Ultimately, the lack of statehood for Taiwan, according to Chen, is the major stumbling block that prevents the implementation of adequate transnational measures to prevent trafficking. Nhatthien Nguyen uses "routine activity theory" and its three components (motivated offenders, suitable targets, lack of capable guardians) to examine East Asian gangs—Chinese Triads, Thai and Vietnamese gangs—and their nefarious activities that include human trafficking for CSE. In the end, Nguyen says, it is the lack of will and recognition of the horrors of human sex trafficking that largely contribute to its excesses in East Asia.

The Europe-Eurasian region is examined through Margaret Melrose's chapter, "Mercenary Territory: A UK Perspective on Human Trafficking," which shows that even though the UK is classified as a Tier 1 country by the United States, the UK is a destination and transit country for trafficking victims. Unless the UK government distinguishes between human smuggling and trafficking and it may serve its legal purpose, in reality it has not helped the trafficked victims who are victimized further by the government's restrictions on asylum applications and crackdown on "illegal" immigrants. Karin Bruckmüller and Stefan Schumann, in their chapter covering Austria, Poland and Croatia reveal on the one hand the advantages of the European Union's circle of laws and human rights frameworks that attempt to put the brakes on human trafficking. On the other hand, problems remain to be still tackled in identification of victims of trafficking and in data collection regionally and internationally.

The region of the Near East is examined by Sunita Manian in "The Wretched of the Earth: Trafficking, the Maghreb and Europe"—a title inspired by Fanon's work—which explores the situation of human sex trafficking in Tunisia, Algeria and Morocco, the three Maghreb countries of Northern Africa. A significant point that Manian raises is how the "economic, social and political interests" of Europe, which serves as destination countries, have shaped the discussion of trafficking rather than the rights of the trafficked victims. Her arguments parallel that of Melrose's previous chapter on the United Kingdom. Manian shows how decolonization or other international financial arrangements such as the IMF's Structural Adjustment Programs offer the "push" factor for individuals to be trafficked to Western Europe. Another chapter that complements the former is Brian Crim's, "Addicted to Cheap Labor: The Gulf States, the Near East, and Trafficking," where Crim uses the "core-dependency" model to investigate the degree of human trafficking in the region. According to this model, the poorer states of the Near East such as Syria, Egypt, Jordan and Lebanon, Iran and Iraq constitute the periphery that is dependent on the richer "core" states such as Kuwait, Oman, Saudi Arabia and the United Arab Emirates. Lured by prospects for domestic employment, women and children get trapped in the racket of human trafficking for CSE.

In covering the South Asian region, Arvind Verma shows that "Trafficking in India" can be traced historically to aristocratic backing of such activity for sexual purposes that began thousands of years ago. The devaluing of women continues in the modern period, with the failure of the police to investigate criminal networks and a lack of rehabilitation efforts for the victims have exacerbated the situation. A somewhat similar situation but more pronounced because of the nascent state of the Kabul government, is presented by Michael Bush who examines the case of "Afghanistan and the Sex Trade." He shows how the extraordinary setting of military conflict and rampant poverty are catalysts for trafficking of women and children for CSE—ironically, the trafficking income finances and sustains the conflict in its own peculiar way.

The Western Hemisphere region is covered by Brad Bullock's chapter, "Sex Traffic and Trafficking in the Caribbean" where he astutely underscores the point that the "Caribbean problem is not so much sex trafficking but rather *sex traffic,* encouraged by strategies to increase revenues from tourism." Highlighting the case of the Dominican Republic, Bullock notes that Caribbean governments' economic plans to stimulate growth through tourism have had the consequence of promoting human sex trafficking rather than stifling it. He adds that perceptions of race, gender, and sex along with persistent global inequalities have contributed to the West's consumption of the sex trade in the Caribbean. Mirna Carranza and Henry Parada focus their attention on the trafficking of children for sexual purposes in their chapter on Central America with an emphasis on Nicaragua. In "Child Commercial Sexual Exploitation in Nicaragua," Carranza and Parada use a critical globalization framework for examining the political economy of sexuality and its relationship to the sex tourism industry. One notices a common thread in Bullock's analyses of the

Caribbean and the Dominican Republic and its similarities to short-sighted neoliberal policies of governments such as that of Nicaragua highlighted by Carranza and Parada.

The North American region is examined first by Kimberly McCabe's chapter "Sex Trafficking in the United States" where McCabe acknowledges the U.S. future to classify itself in the tier classification system as an outcome of their efforts to reduce human trafficking as well as the role of organized crime networks in the country and conflicting jurisdictional boundaries which often hinder the identifications and investigations of sex trafficking cases. Grassano and Ryan in their chapter "Sex Trafficking in Canada: Limited Efforts in Law Enforcement" identify specific roadblocks experienced by Canadian police as they attempt to enforce anti-trafficking legislation in a culture of social diversity. Finally, David Richards's chapter on "Sex Trafficking and Mexico" emphasizes three main reasons for Mexico's problems with human trafficking for CSE: porous borders with the United States, poverty, and corruption that are all closely linked to the narcotics trafficking networks and the fact that Mexico continues to fall behind in its commitment to prevent this criminal activity that lures many Caribbean and Central American women into the country.

As the chapters in the subsequent pages will reveal, while each case of sex trafficking in each region of the world is unique in its own way, there are some common realities that one encounters in the sex trafficking of women and children for commercial sexual purposes. First, the politics of numbers and the quantification itself present a problematic that is not easily resolved. The U.S. State Department's data gathering often are based on information provided by one or two local nongovernmental organizations, when government information may not be forthcoming or sometimes may supplement the host government's documentation. Second, certain social issues that are common include the devaluing of women and the personification of women as objects, gender inequity as well as global inequalities, a material culture that constantly provides the myth of glamour and allure that forces girls and women to seek what appears to be a path to fulfillment. Third, while conflict situations exacerbate the prevalence of trafficking for CSE, non–conflict related venues for sports and entertainment also tend to aggravate trafficking incidences. The following chapters detail sex trafficking from a global perspective.

References

BBC News. "Games May Spark Prostitution Rise." July 14, 2009. <http://news.bbc.co.uk/2/hi/uk_news/england/london/8150364.stm> (10 Nov. 2009).

FBI. (2005). *Involuntary Servitude and Human Trafficking Initiatives.* Feb 22, 2005. <http://miami.fbi.gov/servitude.htm> (10 Nov. 2009)

International Organization for Migration (IOM). (1999). *Perspectives on Trafficking of Migrants: International Organization for Migration Foundation Against Trafficking in Women.* NY: Global Alliance Against Trafficking in Women.

International Organization for Migration (IOM). 2009. *N General Assembly Thematic Dialogue: Taking Collective Action to End Human Trafficking.* NY: UN Headquarters, May 2009. <www.un.org/ga/president/63/interactive/ht/iom.pdf> (10 Nov. 2009)

Interpol. (2004). *People Smuggling.* Lyon, France: Interpol.

McCabe, K. (2008). *The Trafficking of Persons: National and International Responses.* NY: Peter Lang.

Mini Singh. N. "Debate on Trafficking and Sex-Slavery." *The Feminist Sexual Ethics Project* (Brandeis University). www.brandeis.edu/projects/fse/Pages/traffickingdebate.html (10 Nov. 2009)

Munro, V. (2006). "Stopping Traffic? A Comparative Study of Responses to the Trafficking of Women for Prostitution." *British Journal of Criminology,* 46(2), 318–333.

UNICEF. (2009). Children and Conflict in a Changing World: The Machel Study 10 Year Strategic Review, NY: UNICEF Publications. <*www.unicef.org/publications/ files/Machel_Study_10_Year_Strategic_Review_EN_030909.pdf*> (10 Nov. 2009).

U.S. Department of State. (2001). *Trafficking in Persons.* Report. Washington, DC: Office to Monitor and Combat Trafficking in Persons.

U.S. Department of State. (2008). *Trafficking in Persons.* Report. Washington, DC: Office to Monitor and Combat Trafficking in Persons.

United Nations Office on Drugs and Crime (UNODC). (2006, April). *Trafficking in Persons: Global Patterns.* UN: Human Trafficking Unit.

I

AFRICA

Kimberly A. McCabe and Sabita Manian

INATTENTION TO AFRICA IN GENERAL, and African human trafficking cases in particular, has left a vacuum in empirical data for the region:

> Over the last few years there has been a lot of research and work done on trafficking of women from Asia and Eastern Europe, but there has been very little attention paid to African women and children. . . . Because there has been little focus, statistics and data are very hard to come by, however, tens of thousands of people from Africa are believed to be trafficked every year, according to the State Department.
>
> —Don Payne (HoR—NJ), House Subcommittee on Africa

The two chapters in this section—one on Southern Africa and the other on the Horn of Africa—attempt to address the lacuna in attention and scholarly work mentioned by Representative Payne in the above quote. The chapters follow the geographical lead of the U.S. State Department's Bureau of African Affairs in the selection of case studies. The Bureau of African Affairs focuses on countries in Sub-Saharan Africa, but not those of North Africa—the latter set of African countries (Algeria, Egypt, Libya, Morocco, and Tunisia) falls within the purview of the Bureau of Near Eastern Affairs. Technically, the Horn of Africa (Djibouti, Eritrea, Ethiopia, Kenya, and Somalia) comes under the "Sub-Saharan Africa" section.

Whenever the continent of Africa makes it to a news headline, it is to announce devastating and catastrophic news of droughts, famines, genocide, ethnic conflict, tyranny or intraregional wars. The toll of human trafficking, for both domestic labor and sexual exploitation that leads women into the hellish situations within Africa or in the richer states of the West and the Middle East, is heartrending.

> At present, there are several devastating crises that we cannot ignore, including in Congo, Nigeria, the Sahel, Sudan and Zimbabwe. But I believe one region stands out for its particular significance to our national security, and that is the Horn of Africa and specifically the deepening crisis in Somalia . . . where the need for a carefully planned and long-term approach is particularly urgent. (U.S. Senator Russ Feingold on Africa, 2009)

Various calamities, both man-made and natural, have led to not only internal displacement but also external migration of refugees from devastated lands. Women, children, and men who flee their disastrous settings are often the most vulnerable victims of sex trafficking. According to the United Nations, human trafficking is a multibillion dollar per year enterprise and it has been pointed out that the cost of a slave today is far less than what African slaves once fetched in the antebellum United States—a difference owing in part to cheap modern transportation (Kapstein, 2006). Africa had been the locus of the Atlantic slave trade for centuries and while slavery as we knew it has ended, it has taken the avatar in contemporary times, of "modern day slavery," with the trafficking of women and children for both domestic servitude and commercial sexual trade. The indignities of this modern day slavery continues to heap its devastating effects on its victims, even as the process today is aggravated by globalization's political, economic and technological structures.

Out of a total of 52 countries in Africa, 46 of them (compared to 156 countries worldwide) report "adult forced labor"; there are 10 African states out of 25 that have the distinction of being *"Countries of Origin"* for trafficking of children for forced labor; 23 out of 53 African states serve as *"Countries of Origin, Transit and Destination for Trafficking of Children* for Forced Labor and Child Labor Exploitation" and 15 out of 76 countries where Internal Trafficking of Adults for Commercial Sexual Exploitation (CSE) occurs are located in Africa (Protection Project, 2009). The silver lining in this picture are the 15 African countries out of 59 others across the world have comprehensive anti-trafficking laws that focus on preventing and punishing trafficking while protecting the trafficked victims, while 10 African states out of 73 worldwide have active laws that criminalize trafficking (Protection Project).

From 2003 to 2007, the U.S. Department of State reports that there have been nearly 700 prosecutions of human trafficking cases with 237 convictions in Africa. In addition, their conviction rate for human trafficking cases has steadily increased as 30 new or amended legislative actions have been adopted during that same time period; however, prevention efforts on the part of most governments are extremely weak.

A 2009 UNICEF report confirms what others have noted as primary contributors to sex trafficking: poverty, limited work opportunities, lack of governmental infrastructure to provide social services and additional factors that are true for all those countries undergoing violent conflict, viz., "breakdown in community structures" that occur when there is an outbreak in violent conflict which "place[s] young girls especially at risk of sexual exploitation and 'transactional' or 'survival' sex" leading to "enslavement, forced prostitution and rape" (UNICEF, 2009, 36). The two chapters in this section, underscore not only the causal factors for CSE that is universal, i.e., poverty; but they also highlight the increasingly acute vulnerability of victims that are compounded by violent conflict, the problems to resolution of sex trafficking due to lack of government resources such as legal or law enforcement infrastructure, and even data collection difficulties due to handicapped governments overburdened by other domestic issues.

Acknowledged by these researchers is the grand scale of human trafficking to include not only cases of sex and labor trafficking, but also cases of child trafficking for soldiering, adoption, etc. Through writings such as the two included in this section, an attempt is made to identify specific problems within the geographic region of Africa as related to sex trafficking.

References

Committee on International Relations, House of Representatives, Subcommittee on Africa. 2005. Combating Human Trafficking: Achieving Zero Tolerance. <http://commdocs.house.gov/committees/intlrel/hfa99820.000/hfa99820_0f.htm>(15 Oct. 2009).

Congressional Record Statement of U.S. Senator Russ Feingold on Africa, January 27, 2009. <http://feingold.senate.gov/record.cfm?id=307389> (15 Oct. 2009).

Kapstein, Ethan B. (2006) "The New Global Slave Trade." *Foreign Affairs*, 85(6), 103–115

SAIS. (2009). *The Protection Project Review of the Trafficking in Persons Report.* Johns Hopkins University. <www.protectionproject.org/pdf/The%20Protection%20Project%20Review%20of%20the%20TIP%20Report%202009.pdf> (16 Oct. 2009).

UNICEF. (2009). *Children and Conflict in a Changing World the Machel Study 10 Year Strategic Review,* NY: UNICEF Publications. <www.unicef.org/publications/files/Machel_Study_10_Year_Strategic_Review_EN_030909.pdf> (16 Oct. 2009).

2

Sex Trafficking in the Horn of Africa

Sabita Manian

A CONGRESSIONAL TESTIMONY DESCRIBED accurately the state of affairs in the Horn of Africa:

> In addition to drought, which has contributed to near-famine conditions in the Horn during six of the past 10 years, ongoing tension between Ethiopia and Eritrea, prolonged civil and clan conflict in Somalia, and the multifaceted conflict in Ethiopia's Ogaden region continue to drain the human and financial resources of these countries, undermining national and international development efforts and the stability of the region as a whole . . . and the risks our partners face on a daily basis. (Katherine J. Almquist, USAID)

This statement succinctly captures both natural and human made calamities that have underscored the downward spiral of peace and stability in the Horn; and provides the unfortunate scenario under which the notorious trafficking of women and children for sexual exploitation thrives in the region. In the context of intractable conflict that underscores most of Africa and especially the hottest conflict zone in the world, the Horn of Africa (Djibouti, Eritrea, Ethiopia, Kenya, and Somalia), the women and children who are trafficked undergo the dual victimization of the violent conflict environment of their state and the exploitation of their bodies. In addition to the sociopolitical climate that leads to greater vulnerabilities of women and children, national and international criminal networks in cahoots with corrupt public officials aid and abet such human trafficking (Opara, 2007). The situation is exacerbated by the lack of a legitimate government (in the case of Somalia or as in the case of Ethiopia), one that simply does not have the infrastructural wherewithal to deal with the criminal act of human trafficking. In Africa in general, and particularly in Somalia and Ethiopia, child trafficking of children ostentatiously happens for reasons of child labor (U.S. House of Representatives Hearing, 2005) many of whom then subsequently become further victimized sexually and end up becoming affected by the dreaded HIV-AIDS. Thus, the human tragedies emerging from the continent due to this modern day slavery for sexual exploitation persevere to this day.

This chapter will focus on sex trafficking in Somalia, largely because it is a heretofore relatively little explored subject. The case of Somalia will be examined against that of Ethiopia, and the rest of the Horn. First, an account of recent political historic of Somalia will be provided for a better understanding of the complexities of that "failed state" in the region, which make the dynamics of human trafficking that much more pernicious. This will be followed by examining the specific case of Somalia in the context of sex trafficking in the Horn, as described in the *Trafficking in Persons Report* (2008). Next, the U.S. State Department's TIP reports will be assessed for the Horn countries in general and Somalia in particular, for the period from 2000–2007, given the countries' various tier ranking in the same document. Finally, in the concluding section, U.S. aid and relations with the said countries (or the lack of it) in the Horn will be assessed, so as to draw some relationship between the TIP report ranking and U.S. foreign policy involvement. In addressing potential solutions to the global problem of trafficking, the record of successes or failures of local and international efforts will be briefly examined. This chapter relies mostly on news media sources and human rights reports, because as mentioned in the introduction to the region, scant attention has been paid to issues of sex trafficking in Africa and therefore, hardly any books or reliable data on trafficking exist for the continent.

Somalia

[A]n estimated 16,000 people have been killed since the start of 2007, with over 28,000 people wounded and more than one million displaced. USAID now estimates that 3.2 million people—soon to be half of the population—are in need of emergency assistance, including hundreds of thousands of refugees in neighboring countries. The stories and images of human suffering coming out of Somalia are horrifying. (Senator Russ Feingold, 2009)

No one would have predicted that Somalia would descend into such a morass as it has today; certainly not in June 1961, when its future appeared glowing with a new national constitution that signaled Somalia's sovereign democratic statehood. Everything seemed set in the right direction for the nascent state especially when in 1969, the government of Mohammed Ibrahim Egal renounced pan-Somali nationalism (which would have meant constant conflict with its neighbors) and instead made positive overtures to Djibouti, Ethiopia and Kenya. Ethiopia, a traditional foe of Somalia, rejected the outstretched hand and thereby contributed to the Somali military's nationalist fury (Ethiopia's rebuttal was seen as a source of dishonor) against the civilian government which resulted in a coup in October 1969 that brought Major General Mohammed Siad Barre as president. Siad Barre's military rule along with Superpower politics of the Cold War sounded a death knell for the budding democracy. The following two decades of the seventies and eighties saw both Somalia and Ethiopia as pawns in the Superpowers' game as they battled one another. The 1977–1978 Ogaden War was followed in the 1980s by an Ethiopian invasion into Somalia. While Soviet military advisers were influencing the Haile Merriam regime in Ethiopia, Washington befriended Siad Barre who had by then rejected his "scientific socialism" (Human Rights Watch, 2007: 10–12; U.S. Dept. of State, 2009). Meantime, internecine inter-ethnic conflict in Somalia was all pervasive through the 1980s, leading to a flood of refugees fleeing the violence who poured into the neighboring states of Ethiopia, Djibouti, and Kenya.

The post–Cold War 1990s saw a segment of northeastern Somalia—Puntland—an arid part of the land, declare itself an autonomous state in 1998 (Bradbury, 129–131). Unlike its neighbor to the west, Somaliland, they did not wish for recognition as a sovereign independent entity (BBC, April 2009). Somaliland, a semi-arid region along the Gulf of Aden, declared its independence after the overthrow of the former military dictator, Siad Barre. While Somaliland continues to claim international recognition as a sovereign state, the international community has not done so. Meantime, Puntland and Somaliland have been forcefully contesting two pieces of territory, Sanaag and Sool (Bradbury, 50–53, 197–199) leading to increased militia and paramilitary activities—the immediate victims of which are civilians.

The 1990s thus saw Somalia fragmented with escalating violence, the famous "Black Hawk Down" scenario that signaled (a) the end of U.S. humanitarian intervention and state-building; and (b) consequently, a lack of a viable government in Mogadishu, which continues to be mired in violence and statelessness. According to a Human Rights Watch (HRW) report, the Ethiopian invasion of Somalia in late 2006 led to a "human rights and humanitarian catastrophe imperiling millions of Somalis (2008)." The invasion was compounded by further intraethnic fighting so that "some 6,000 civilians are estimated to have been killed in Mogadishu and across southern and central Somalia in 2007" (*Congressional Testimony*, Lynn Frederiksson).

MAP 2.1
Somalia

Source: U.S. Department of State website

Amidst this national fragmentation and cross-border conflict, Somali women refugees often bore the brunt of the economic and political upheaval and subsequent sexual malady as they fled across the border, either to seek an outlet to safety or a source of work elsewhere—this passage would have to be conducted through soliciting human smugglers. At the Global Tribunal of Violation of Women's Human Rights in Vienna (1993), a Somali woman refugee testified that even "when they are trying to get legalized status in the neighboring countries or in developed countries, quite often men have to pay with bribes and women have to pay with sex" (Asale Angel-Ajani, 297). In the decade or more since this testimony, little if anything has changed for Somali women.

As the anti-trafficking advocacy center, the Protection Project at Johns Hopkins University notes, Somalia serves primarily as a source country for sex trafficking where women are trafficked to the Middle East, Europe and to other countries within Africa itself. Since children in Somalia and other parts of Africa are not registered at birth, it is easier for them to be moved across borders or even for adults to be smuggled outside of Somalia. The lawlessness that has resulted in Somalia and its fragmented units, has led the waters of the Gulf of Aden (notorious for high sea piracies) to be one of the main channels for trafficking women to Yemen and from there on to Europe or other parts of the Middle East. Somalia "represents a major area of transit for people being smuggled from the Horn of Africa, particularly Ethiopians, to the Gulf States. . . . Puntland is reported to be one of the world's busiest smuggling hubs" (IOM, *Somalia*). Amira Ali Mohammed, a trafficked Somali woman, who wanted to remove herself from the perils of Mogadishu and find work in Saudi Arabia recounted her tale:

> In the early hours of the morning, on the way to the boat, the man and his companion dragged her off and attacked her . . . the 22-year-old, who had fled fighting in the capital, recalled: "They suddenly got hold of my arms and started to drag me away. . . . I wanted to work as a maid in Saudi Arabia, they pay you well there. The money was given by my parents, now I have no more money and I am stuck here in this place [refugee camp in Boosaso, Puntland]. I cannot go back to Mogadishu, it is too dangerous." (*The Independent*, May 25, 2006)

Discussing a similar situation in Boosaso, Puntland, an IOM official recalled: "I have recently dealt with the case of a 17-year-old girl who was going to catch a boat. She was sleeping in a shed on the beach when she was taken away. She was gang raped by nine men. She died" (*The Independent*, May 25, 2006).

Somalia and its fragmented parts serve as a source, transit, and destination for trafficked women and children, who undergo both variants of trafficking, internal (to the Horn) and transnational. The transnational trafficking of humans that benefits traffickers in various parts of Somalia (including Puntland and Somaliland) goes hand in hand with maritime piracy, where the pirates who are well armed and well-financed work in league with paramilitary forces, militias and political leaders (Shiiq, 2007). The Transitional Federal Government (TFG) in Mogadishu watches as armed militias traffic women and children to the United Arab Emirates, "for commercial sexual exploitation" while "Ethiopian women are trafficked to and through Somalia to the Middle East (Iraq, Lebanon, Syria) for forced labor and sexual exploitation." The Mogadishu transitional government and the Puntland authorities are not only "silent spectators . . . some reliable sources also allege the leaders of Puntland take a lion's share from the revenues of this human trafficking (Ali, 2008)." Child prostitution is not unknown in Somalia. As with the women, Somali children are "trafficked for forced labor and sexual exploitation by armed militias" and other organized syndicates who traffic them to South Africa (U.S. Department of Labor Report, 2006), or to Djibouti in the Horn (TIP Report, 2007), Saudi Arabia and other Middle East countries (including Yemen) either to work as domestic laborers or for begging; and sometimes the parents are complicit in the trafficking of the child (HRW, 2008b). In places like Qatar, trafficked Somali children serve as camel jockeys (TIP, 2004, 201). To make matters worse, Saudi Arabia began deporting trafficked foreign children who had been forced into begging, to Somalia, regardless of their origin. In Somalia, these children are recruited by various militias to fight as child soldiers; making Somalia a destination for trafficked children (HRW, 2008c, 72). Trafficked girl children are even more vulnerable, when repatriated to places like Somalia or Sudan (HRW, 2008c). Some Somali children who reach European countries like Greece either voluntarily flee the violence in their own land and then become victims of trafficking for domestic labor or sex work, or are trafficked (HRW, 2008d, 88, 12).

For the last several years, Somalia has been a "Special Case" in the *Trafficking in Persons* reports, because of a "lack of viable government since 1991" (TIP, 2009); though in some instances of the reports (2001, 2002) data have simply been unavailable (see Table 2.1) because of any or all of the following: "no U.S. diplomatic presence in the country, the society is closed, there is no

TABLE 2.1
Country Rankings (2001–2008)

Horn of Africa Countries	TIP 2001	TIP 2002	TIP 2003	TIP 2004	TIP 2005	TIP 2006	TIP 2007	TIP 2008
Djibouti	n.a	n.a	n.a	n.a.	Special Case	Tier 2 Watch List	Tier 2 Watch List	Tier 2
Eritrea*	n.a	n.a	n.a	n.a.	n.a.	n.a.	n.a.	n.a.
Ethiopia	Tier 2	Tier 2	Tier 2	Tier 2 Watch List	Tier 2	Tier 2	Tier 2	Tier 2
Kenya	n.a	n.a	Tier 2	Tier 2 Watch List	Tier 2	Tier 2 Watch List	Tier 2 Watch List	Tier 2
Somalia	n.a	n.a	Special Case	Special Case	Special Case	Special Case	Special Case	Special Case

Source: Trafficking in Persons Reports, 2001–2008
* It was not until 2009 that Eritrea began to be ranked in the TIP Report.

free press, or few NGOs operate in the country" (TIP, 2002, 12). However, since 2003 a section termed "Special Cases" was introduced to evaluate these very countries despite the conditions mentioned above. As mentioned earlier, Somalia's trafficking situation is best evaluated against the record of its neighbors, more importantly Ethiopia.

Ethiopia

Ethiopia was described thus by U.S. Senator Russ Feingold (Wisconsin): "Ethiopia sits on the Horn of Africa—perhaps one of the roughest neighborhoods in the world, with Somalia a failed state . . . Eritrea an inaccessible authoritarian regime that exacerbates conflicts throughout the region . . . and now Kenya descending into crisis" (*Congressional Statement*, March 2008). Surrounded by such gross instability, nearly 30,000 teenage Ethiopian girls get trafficked annually to Lebanon from where they are transported mainly to other parts of the Middle East either for sexual labor or "forced domestic labor" (*Congressional Hearing*, Shirley Barnes, 2005). Victims from Ethiopia may end up in Bahrain, Djibouti, Kuwait, Lebanon, Syria, Sudan and Yemen either for domestic servitude or ultimately end up as sex workers via Lebanon in Turkey, Italy and Greece.

The internal trafficking of children in Ethiopia has been documented by ECPAT (End Child Prostitution and Trafficking), a global network of advocacy organizations: Ethiopian children and children trafficked from other Horn countries, especially Somalia, are used for commercial sexual purposes in nightclubs and bars or "simply stand on street corners waiting for men to pick them up" (ECPAT, 2007). However, with regards to "trafficking for sexual purposes, related data usually collates women and children, and it is difficult to say with certainty to what extent children in particular are affected" (ECPAT, 2007, 12). While the sale price for an Ethiopian child is a meager US$1.20 to work as prostitutes or domestic servants, "nearly 20,000 children, some 10 years old, are sold each year by their parents and trafficked . . . [about] two-thirds of the children are trafficked by brokers who take a percentage of the child's earnings, while one-third are trafficked by friends and family (UK Home Office, 123)." For these reasons, Ethiopia, has continued to be ranked as Tier 2 from 2001–2008—except for 2004 when it was placed on a Tier 2 Watch List when the government had not fully complied with the Trafficking Victims Protection Act's (TVPA) minimum standards and for a dramatic increase in the number of trafficked victims. By 2005, Ethiopia swung back to its original status of a Tier 2 ranking. With the tourism industry picking up in Ethiopia in recent years, sex trafficking is serving as a more lucrative business.

Djibouti

Djibouti is an East African country by the Gulf of Aden that hosts a U.S. military base. This coastal republic boasts a population of about 650,000 that is of majority Somali and Afar ethnicities and is mostly Muslim; additionally there are nearly 150,000 foreigners a majority of whom are French including 3000 French troops (*Background Notes*, 2009). Lack of documentation of trafficking in Djibouti did not deter the U.S. State Department authorities to rank it as a "Special Case" in 2005, despite the "dearth of solid evidence" and with mere reliance on "anecdotal evidence" (TIP, 2005, 104). Women from Ethiopia and Somalia are trafficked to Djibouti which serves as a transit or destination place. Children from neighboring African states fall prey to prostitution rings in Djibouti and these child prostitutes work in the brothels, streets or from apartments run by pimps. In 2006, the government recognized human trafficking as a problem; when it did, it was the United States that rewarded Djibouti for "significant efforts" at tackling trafficking by being elevated to a Tier 2 Watch List status, though it fell short of the minimum steps required by the U.S. State Department (TIP, 2006, 108) and had increasing numbers of trafficked cases. It has been recommended that the government work in league with local NGOs to initiate a procedure for the provision of "protective services" to victims of trafficking (TIP, 2007, 93). The following year, 2008, Djibouti went to Tier 2 status—a promotion for not having an augmentation of trafficking incidents and for having a slightly better record of apprehending 5 French nationals for child sexual abuse allegations (TIP, 2008, 108).

Kenya

Kenya is a source, transit and destination country for human trafficking. Kenyan women and children are trafficked to the Middle East (Saudi Arabia, Lebanon, the U.A.E.) and to Europe (mostly to Germany); women from India, China and Pakistan are trafficked via Nairobi before they end in the brothels of Europe; while children are trafficked to Kenyan towns from not only the Horn countries of Ethiopia and Somalia, but also from Uganda, Rwanda and the Democratic Republic of Congo—girls are made to work as barmaids and then coerced into sexual work (TIP, 2008, 157). At the 2006 World Cup Soccer venue Kenyan authorities noted that women from that country had begun to be trafficked to Germany for the games (Congressional Statement, Katherine Chon, 2006). Otherwise, women trafficked from Kenya are made to journey from Poland to Austria, Belgium, Denmark, Germany, Greece, Italy, the Netherlands, Spain, Sweden, and Japan for commercial sexual exploitation. Kenya's case is somewhat similar to that of its other Horn neighbors: nearly 10,000 to 15,000 girls are trafficked to Kenya for prostitution while child sex tourism has become widespread (TIP, 2008, 36).

Conclusion

The case of Somalia has revealed that in order to begin tackling the monstrosity of human trafficking in the country, the very first step is the establishment of some political and economic order and stability in Mogadishu. Since Somalia is mired in lawlessness and lack of legitimacy, Somali women and children cannot rely on domestic or nongovernmental institutions for support. Yet, since October 2008, U.S. Agency for International Development (USAID) has partnered with FAO, Mercy Corps, Medair Swiss, International Red Cross, UNICEF, CARE, etc. to accelerate their nonmilitary aid to Somalia (USAID, 2009).

The move by USAID to integrate governmental efforts with other humanitarian agencies is an accurate one, but unless Ethiopia and Somalia come to a peaceful understanding, aid and development cannot be sustained. This bilateral relation was much stymied when the Bush administration recognized Ethiopia as a partner on the "War on Terror" thereby motivating Addis Ababa to invade Somalia in 2006—leaving the civilian population vulnerable to the vagaries of violence and traffickers. The greater the instability in Somalia, the more of a breeding ground it will be for terrorist activities and for trafficking. Instead, if the Somali moderate Islamic government in exile of President Sheikh Sharif Sheikh Ahmed can be supported in their battle against the Al Shabab militia (which the United States accuses of having ties with Al Qaeda), there is a ray of hope for the Somalis—the European Union, the United States, and the African Union must all be on board to forge this positive dynamic. Furthermore, to the political solution must be added a sociological one, viz., education of boys and girls about the value of women and their contribution to society will be an important long-term strategy to combat the demeaning and the victimization of women and children. There is no one magic potion for the ills of human trafficking but an effort can be made, locally, regionally and multilaterally to gradually change the ignoble exercise of the sex trade.

References

Abdirhahman, A. (2008). "Puntland: Human Cargo Trade out of Bosasso." *Somaliland Times*, (313). <www.somalilandtimes.net/sl/2008/313/05.shtml> (7 Nov. 2009).

Angel-Ajani, A., "Displacing Diaspora: Trafficking African Women and Transnational Practices." (2006). In Michael A. Gomez's (ed) *Diasporic Africa*. NY: New York University Press, 290–308.

BBC News. (2009, April). "Puntland," <http://news.bbc.co.uk/2/hi/africa/country_profiles/4276288.stm> (7 Nov. 2009).

Bradbury, M. (2008). *Becoming Somaliland*. IN: Indiana University Press.

ECPAT. (2007). *Global Monitoring Report against Commercial Sexual Exploitation of Children: Ethiopia*. <www.ecpat.net/A4A_2005/PDF/AF/Global_Monitoring_Report-ETHIOPIA.pdf> (7 Nov. 2009).

Ethiopian Review. (2008). "U.S. Senate Schedules Hearing on Horn of Africa," March 9, 2008. <www.ethiopianreview.com/content/2048> (7 Nov. 2009).

Hearing before the Subcommittee on Africa, Global Human Rights and International Operations of the Committee on International Relations. (March 9, 2005). Statement of the Honorable Shirley E. Barnes, Former U.S. Ambassador to the Republic of Madagascar, "Combating Human Trafficking: Achieving Zero Tolerance," Serial No. 109–132, p. 44.

Human Rights Watch (henceforth HRW). (2007). *Shell Shocked: Civilians Under Siege in Mogadishu*. <www.hrw.org/en/reports/2007/08/12/shell-shocked-0> (7 Nov. 2009).

HRW. (2008a). *So Much to Fear: War Crimes and the Devastation of Somalia*. <www.hrw.org/en/reports/2008/12/08/so-much-fear> (7 Nov. 2009).

HRW. (2008b). *Adults Before Their Time*. <www.hrw.org/sites/default/files/reports/saudicrd0308_1.pdf> (7 Nov. 2009).

HRW. (2008c). *Saudi Arabia: Heavy Price of Unfair Justice System*. <www.hrw.org/en/news/2008/03/23/saudi-arabia-heavy-price-unfair-justice-system> 7 Nov. 2009).

HRW. (2008d). *Left to Survive*. <www.hrw.org/sites/default/files/reports/greece-1208web_0.pdf> (7 Nov. 2009).

The Independent. (May 25, 2006). "Human Trafficking: Greed and the Trail of Death." <www.independent.co.uk/news/world/africa/human-trafficking-greed-and-the-trail-of-death-479640.html> (7 Nov. 2009).

Jaye, T. (2008). "The Security Culture of the ECOWAS: Origins, Development and the Challenge of Child Trafficking." *Journal of Contemporary African Studies*, 26(2): 151–168.

Kapstein, B. (2006). "The New Global Slave Trade." *Foreign Affairs*, 85(6): 103–115.

Nhema, A., and Tiyambe Zeleza, P. (2008). *The Roots of African Conflicts: the Causes & Costs*. Ohio University Press.

Opara, V. (2007). "Emerging Issues in the Trafficking of African Women for Prostitution," in T. Falola and Afolabi, N. (eds) *The Human Cost of African Migrations*. Routledge: 165–220.

Prendergast, J. and Thomas-Jensen, C. (2007). "Blowing the Horn." *Foreign Affairs*, 86(2): 59–74.

Shiiq, S. (2007). "Puntland: The Epicenter of Somalia's Piracy and Human Trafficking." *Somali Times*, Is. 310: <www.somalilandtimes.net/sl/2007/310/23.shtml> (7 Nov. 2009).

Statement of Ms. Katherine Chon, Hearing Before the House Subcommittee on Africa, Global Human Rights and International Operations, "Germany's World Cup Brothels: 40,000 Women and Children at Risk of Exploitation through Trafficking." May 4, 2006, Serial No. 109–178.

Swan, J, U.S. Deputy Asst. Secretary for African Affairs. (2007). "U.S. Policy in the Horn of Africa." Speech to the 4th Ethiopian Development Studies Conference, Michigan, 2007. <www.state.gov/p/af/rls/rm/90573.htm> (7 Nov. 2009).

UK Home Office. (2007). *Ethiopia.* <www.ecoi.net/file_upload/1329_1200047901_ ethiopia-210207.pdf> (7 Nov. 2009).

USAID. (2009). *Somalia: Complex Emergency.* <www.usaid.gov/our_work/humanitarian_assistance/disaster_assistance/countries/somalia/template/fs_sr/fy2009/somalia_ce_sr04_01-15-2009.pdf> (7 Nov. 2009).

U.S. Congressional Statement of Senator Russ Feingold on Africa. (January 2009). <http://feingold.senate.gov/record.cfm?id=307389> (7 Nov. 2009).

U.S. Congressional Statement of Senator Russ Feingold on the Political Crisis in Ethiopia (March 3, 2008). <http://feingold.senate.gov/record.cfm?id=305900> (7 Nov. 2009).

U.S. Congressional Testimony of Katherine J. Almquist, Assistant Administrator for Africa, (USAID), before the Senate Foreign Relations Subcommittee on African Affairs, March 11, 2008, "Evaluating U.S. Policy Objectives and Options on the Horn of Africa." <www.senate.gov/~foreign/testimony/2008/AlmquistTestimony080311a.pdf> (7 Nov. 2009).

U.S. Congressional Testimony by Lynn Fredriksson, Advocacy Director for Africa, Amnesty International USA, March 11, 2008 <www.senate.gov/~foreign/testimony/2008/FredrikssonTestimony080311a.pdf> (7 Nov. 2009).

U.S. Department of State. *Background Note: Somalia.* March 2009: <www.state.gov/r/pa/ei/bgn/2863.htm> (7 Nov. 2009).

U.S. Department of State. (2001). *Victims of Trafficking and Violence Protection Act of 2000: Trafficking in Persons Report, 2001.* <www.state.gov/g/tip/rls/tiprpt/2001/> (7 Nov. 2009).

U.S. Department of State. (2002). *Victims of Trafficking and Violence Protection Act of 2000: Trafficking in Persons Report, 2002.* <www.state.gov/documents/organization/10815.pdf> (7 Nov. 2009).

U.S. Department of State. (2003, June). *Trafficking in Persons.* Report. Washington, DC: Office to Monitor and Combat Trafficking in Persons.

U.S. Department of State. (2004, June). *Trafficking in Persons.* Report. Washington, DC: Office to Monitor and Combat Trafficking in Persons.

U.S. Department of State. (2005, June). *Trafficking in Persons.* Report. Washington, DC: Office to Monitor and Combat Trafficking in Persons.

U.S. Department of State. (2006, June). *Trafficking in Persons.* Report. Washington, DC: Office to Monitor and Combat Trafficking in Persons.

U.S. Department of State. (2007, June). *Trafficking in Persons.* Report. Washington, DC: Office to Monitor and Combat Trafficking in Persons.

U.S. Department of State. (2008, June). *Trafficking in Persons.* Report. Washington, DC: Office to Monitor and Combat Trafficking in Persons.

U.S. Department of State. (2009). *Background Notes: Djibouti,* January 2009. <http://www.state.gov/r/pa/ei/bgn/5482.htm> (7 Nov. 2009).

U.S. Department of Labor Report. (2006). *Somalia: Incidence and Nature of Child Labor* <www.dol.gov/ilab/media/reports/tda/tda2006/Somalia.pdf> (7 Nov. 2009).

U.S. House of Representatives Hearing Before the Subcommittee on Africa, Global Human Rights and International Operations. "Combating Human Trafficking: Achieving Zero Tolerance." Prepared Statement of the Hon. Donald Payne, New Jersey, March 9, 2005. <http://hirc.house.gov/archives/109/99820.PDF> (7 Nov. 2009).

3

Sex Trafficking in the Countries of South Africa, Mozambique, and Zimbabwe

William J. Mathias and Kimberly A. McCabe

O NE OF THE EARLIEST THEORIES of migration suggests individuals migrate from one area to another for economic reasons and that the volume of migration decreases as distance increases (Ravenstein, 1889). Although this theory was originally applied to voluntary migration, it may also be applied to forced migration and help to explain common problems within migrant populations of adjacent countries. Specifically, this chapter will focus on the shared criminal problem of sex trafficking among the adjacent countries of South Africa, Mozambique, and Zimbabwe.

South Africa

The Republic of South Africa (hereafter S. Africa) is located at the southern tip of the continent of Africa with the country of Zimbabwe to its north and the country of Mozambique to its east. S. Africa is a country with approximately 470 thousand square miles, a 2008 population of approximately 48 million people, and a density of approximately 100 residents per square mile. In S. Africa, the annual income is approximately $6,000 and there exists a high degree of income inequality with a few residents earning very high incomes and the majority of the country earning little or no income. Finally, few of the women in the country of S. Africa are educated as educational resources are generally spent on the males within the country.

Within the last few years, the country of S. Africa has emerged as a society of significance. Political violence in S. Africa has been greatly reduced, its economy has become more diversified, and government officials are working toward improving the educational system. However, cultural norms change slowly and the norms associated with the oppression of women and the dominance of a male-centered society continues within S. Africa. South Africa continues to be a country with the growing criminal problem of sex trafficking.

South Africa is a source, transit, and destination country for the sex trafficking of women and children. An early BBC (2000) report concluded that since the country of S. Africa became a democracy in 1994, there has been an increase in the abduction of women and children. This problem has continued as many of the victims of abduction are sold to S. Africans and foreigners for sex. Some victims are held prisoner by their traffickers and often tattooed with his name for quick identification of ownership. Since 2001, S. Africa has been placed on either a Tier 2 or Tier 2 Watch list as they do not fully comply with the minimum standards for the elimination of human trafficking. In addition, South Africa is increasingly emerging as a destination country for the trafficking of children for sexual exploitation (UNESCO, 2006).

The U.S. Department of State (2008) suggests that S. Africa's government has demonstrated minimal progress in ending human trafficking through prevention efforts. Whereas the country has initiated several task forces and anti-trafficking efforts, there exists little progress in terms of reported outcomes and country-wide awareness programs. Finally, specific anti-trafficking legislation is nonexistent.

Mozambique

The Republic of Mozambique (hereafter Mozambique) is a country located in southeastern Africa with S. Africa to its southwest and Zimbabwe to its west. Mozambique is a country with approximately 310 thousand square miles, a 2008 population of approximately 22 million people, and a density of approximately 65 residents per square mile. In Mozambique, the annual income is approximately $850, there exists a moderate degree of income inequality, and few females are educated.

Many researchers would consider the country of Mozambique to exist with a weak state structure with periods of transitional party changes providing an environment conducive to the spread of criminal activity (UNESCO, 2006). Daily armed conflicts occur within the country which damage the national economy and provide the push for mass population movements. Military conflicts promote survival strategies and women and children are increasingly vulnerable to victimization. The migration, which results as a response to the military conflicts, is large in the numbers of women and children with these refugee populations at risk for victimization by traffickers.

Mozambique is a source and destination country for the sex trafficking of women and children. Although not ranked in 2001and 2002, since 2003 Mozambique has been placed on either a Tier 2 or Tier 2 Watch list as they also do not fully comply with the minimum standards for the elimination of human trafficking.

In Mozambique and other similar countries, trafficking is the link between supply and demand. For the traffickers, the process is well organized. Those individuals trafficking others for sexual exploitation face a very low risk of arrest or prosecution. Traffickers are well aware of the lack of anti-slavery laws and the corruption of the judicial system; hence the criminal activity flourishes (Fitzgibbons, 2003). Much of the trafficking within Mozambique is controlled by transnational organized crime syndicates or by organized Mozambican refugees living in South Africa (Indian Ocean, 2004); therefore, without strong cross-border cooperation among law enforcement authorities, efforts to control human trafficking are minimal.

The U.S. Department of State (2008) suggests that Mozambique does not fully comply with the minimum standards for the elimination of trafficking. The Mozambique government has experienced the negative publicity associated with public officials suspected of accepting bribes to overlook crimes of human trafficking and limited resources have been made available to protect victims. Finally, Mozambique has not initiated a nationwide public awareness campaign; thus, citizens and, in some cases police, have limited knowledge on the illegal activity of sex trafficking.

Zimbabwe

The Republic of Zimbabwe (hereafter Zimbabwe) is also located in the southern part of Africa with S. Africa to the south and Mozambique to the east. Zimbabwe is a country with approximately 150 square miles, a 2008 population of approximately 13 million people, and a density of approximately 85 residents per square mile. In Zimbabwe, the annual income is approximately $200, there exists a high degree of income inequality and, just as the cases in S. Africa and Mozambique, few females are educated.

In Zimbabwe and other similar countries, children abandoned because of accusations of witchcraft are common. These children are vulnerable to traffickers as they are essentially street children, who beg, steal, and prostitute themselves to survive (ECPAT-UK, 2008). The belief that children can be possessed by evil spirits is widespread in the country; however, the limited research on this phenomenon suggests that the children are labeled as witches as a result of a change in their family dynamics, extreme poverty, the death of a parent, etc. In other words, unwanted children are labeled witches as a reason to explain why they are no longer welcomed into their own homes.

Zimbabwe is a source, transit, and destination country for the sex trafficking of women and children. In addition, Zimbabwe is one of the most central transit points for regional human trafficking. Since 2003, Zimbabwe has been placed on Tier 2, Tier 3, and Tier 2 Watch lists as they do not fully comply with the minimum standards for the elimination of human trafficking. It is suggested that Zimbabwe is the specific transit country for the sex trafficking of individuals from Mozambique into South Africa (UNICEF, 2003). Finally, in 2006, spokespersons from the U.S. White House reported that Zimbabwe was subject to U.S. sanctions because of the government's failure to take steps to halt human trafficking (Humantrafficking.org, 2006).

The U.S. Department of State (2008) reports the country of Zimbabwe does not fully comply with the minimum standards for the elimination of human trafficking. In addition, the trafficking situation in the country has become worse as economic growth has declined and the desire for large-scale migration out of the country has increased. Finally, there is a general lack of understanding about trafficking across citizens and the government's officials.

Sex Trafficking Factors

Within the three closely related countries of S. Africa, Mozambique, and Zimbabwe, three general factors exists which facilitate sex trafficking. Those factors are poverty, child and female oppression, limited border security, and sexual myths. As previously stated, all three of the countries are extremely poor with the majority of their residents living in poverty with little support for educational or medical programs. In addition, in all three countries women and young girls are victims of gender inequality. They are not educated, not valued, sold as wives, and often times viewed as disposable property (International Organization for Migration, 2003). The two practices of Lobolo and Kupita Kufa demonstrate the powerlessness of women in these countries. Lobolo entails a future husband, paying a sum of money or goods to a family in exchange for a wife, to replace his wife with her younger sister if the wife does not please him sexually. The practice of Kupita Kufa requires a widow to sleep with her husband's brother immediately after the death of her husband to gain acceptance into the brother's household. Without a doubt, the desire for money and the roles of women in S. Africa, Mozambique, and Zimbabwe are some of the factors that contribute to the supply and demand to lay the framework for engagements into the criminal activity of sex trafficking.

Other elements as identified by the United Nations Educational, Scientific, and Cultural Organization [UNESCO] (2006) related to the conditions of women, poverty, and the demand for sex trafficking in S. Africa, Mozambique, and Zimbabwe include the growth of the sex industry in those countries and its perceived 'necessary evil' to satisfy the sexual desires of the men in the countries, the low risk nature of sex trafficking as facilitated by the criminal justice systems' lack of desire to arrest and prosecute those involved in trafficking, the ease in controlling the female victims of sex trafficking, the lack of legitimate employment and educational opportunities for women, the general devaluing of women and children within the cultures, and the tolerance of violence against women within the three countries. As cutbacks continue to exist in government services and subsidies, women in poverty will continue to seek ways to increase their income sources, those involved in sex trafficking will continue to identify victims (Truong, 2006).

The third factor which facilitates sex trafficking in South Africa, Mozambique, and Zimbabwe is limited control of the borders. In comparison to the cases of U.S.-Mexico and U.S.-Canada borders, movement across borders of these African countries is largely unregulated and unpatrolled. Limited financial resources largely prohibit the military's and law enforcement's abilities to monitor the movements of individuals within and outside of the countries' jurisdictional lines. Essentially, in countries such as these, where individuals often struggle to feed their families, little or no effort is placed on limiting the movements of those who choose to travel outside of their country borders to seek employment. Of course, as we are aware, individuals move across borders for not only legitimate reasons (e.g., jobs) but also illegitimate reasons (e.g., drug trade and human trafficking).

The fourth factor which facilitates sex trafficking within the countries of S. Africa, Mozambique, and Zimbabwe is a myth related to the HIV virus and AIDS. In all three of the countries of interest, AIDS continues to be a problem as more and more people die from the disease everyday. In these African cultures it is important that men have frequent sex with different partners, this of course, increases the likelihood of the spread of the HIV virus. In an attempt to rid themselves of the HIV virus, many men will force a young, virgin, girl to participate in the ceremony of Okaka. This Okaka entails the infected man to have unprotected sex with the girl to rid himself of the disease. Once the young girl has participated in sexual relations with a man, she is worthless from a cultural perspective. Therefore, she is often at the mercy of pimps or sex traffickers for support. The young girl, HIV positive or negative, is trafficked throughout the countries for sexual exploitation (McCabe, 2008).

In 2003, UNICEF identified several different routes for the transportation of sex trafficking victims within the three countries of South Africa, Mozambique, and Zimbabwe. The first is from Mozambique through Zimbabwe, and into South Africa with transportation also moving in the opposite direction. The second route is from Zimbabwe into South Africa with transportation also occurring in the opposite direction. The third route is from Mozambique to South Africa with transportation in the opposite direction. The fourth route is from Zimbabwe into Mozambique. It is suggested that access to the countries is a consequence of organized crime connections and the complicity of the border authorities (UNESCO, 2006). It is suggested that many of these victims of sex trafficking are destined for prosperous countries such as the United Kingdom and the United States (McCabe, 2008).

As suggested by Hughes (2001), in the large crime networks for sex trafficking, individuals involved rarely know all of the members of the organization and commonly know only their specific contacts. This structure of unknown members often eliminate law enforcement's abilities to identify many members of the network; thus, their efforts are generally focused on two or three individuals when the size of the criminal organization could number over 100 people involved in the activity of sex trafficking.

Efforts to Reduce Sex Trafficking

Attempts to reduce sex trafficking have been initiated in each of the three countries. In the country of S. Africa, the specific problem of child sex tourism has been identified. In response, the military has initiated awareness campaigns targeted toward South African troops deployed on peacekeeping missions. Through these campaigns, soldiers are provided information on issues related to sexual exploitation prior to their deployment. In addition, the South African Police Service has designated a Human Trafficking Desk within its Organized Crime Unit. Research suggests that organized crime is a part of human trafficking; thus, reducing organized crime will reduce human trafficking. Finally, S. Africa utilizes two legislative actions, the Prevention of Organized Crime Act and the recent December 2007 Sexual Offenses Amendment Act to arrest and prosecute those individuals involved in the trafficking of persons.

In the country of Mozambique, some nongovernment organizations (NGOs) have hosted anti-trafficking themes events to include the 2007 anti-child trafficking event in Ressano Garcia to celebrate the Day of the Child. Also in 2007, the Ministry of Interior expanded the number of police stations with offices dedicated to investigating the victimization of women and children. Finally, one-day trafficking seminars have been provided to new police recruits within the central provinces.

In the country of Zimbabwe, the association of problems among adjacent countries is acknowledged. In 2007, Zimbabwe's Interpol Office's Human Trafficking Desk began taking part in international human trafficking investigations to reduce the transportation of trafficking victims. In 2008, the government signed a memorandum of understanding with the South African government for a joint project to regulate the status of illegal immigrants. During the same year, all government controlled radio stations aired public service announcements on human trafficking in multiple languages during their peak migration period.

Conclusion

The countries of South Africa, Mozambique, and Zimbabwe share many common characteristics. Each country is considered, by American standards, to be a poor country, each country's government has identified the need for improvement in their educational system, and each country has documented the criminal activity of sex trafficking within its borders. All three countries have made some attempt to reduce human trafficking although none of the three countries fully comply with the minimum standards for the elimination of human trafficking. As Ravenstein's (1889) theory suggests, adjacent countries such as S. Africa, Mozambique, and Zimbabwe share common migrant populations; therefore, it is reasonable that they also share the common problems associated with those populations. Through efforts which view these countries not as individual units but as a collective structure, this region in Africa may begin to address and reduce sex trafficking.

References

BBC News. (2000). "S. Africa's Child Sex Trafficking Nightmare." *BBC News* November 23, 2000. <http://news.bbc.co.uk/2/hi/africa/1037215.stm> (20 March 2009).

ECPAT-UK. (2008). "Vulnerability and Control of Africa Child Victims of Trafficking UK Experience." *Discussion Paper* (Winter 2008). Grosvenor Gardens, London: Grosvenor Gardens House.

Fitzgibbons, K. (2003). "Modern Day Slavery? The Scope of Trafficking in Persons in Africa." *African Security Review, 12*(1), 1–12.

Hughes, D. (2001). "The Natasha Trade: Transnational Sex Trafficking." *National Institute of Justice,* 246 (January 2001), pp. 9–14.

Humantrafficking.org. (2006). "US Says Zimbabwe Subject to Sanctions." News and Updates (October 9, 2006). <http://humantrafficking.org/updates/428> (20 March 2009).

Indian Ocean. (2004). "Child Trafficking between Mozambique and South Africa." Indian Ocean Newsletter, 17 (January 2004).

International Organization for Migration [IOM]. (2003). *Seduction, Sale and Slavery: Trafficking of Women and Children for Sexual Exploitation in Southern Africa.* NY: Global Alliance Against Trafficking in Women.

McCabe, K. (2008). *The Trafficking of Persons: National and International Responses.* NY: Peter Lang.

Ravenstein, E. (1889). "The Laws of Migration." *Journal of Royal Statistical Society,* 52: 41.

Truong, T. (2006). *Poverty, Gender, and Human Trafficking in Sub-Saharan Africa.* UNESCO: Innocenti Research Centre.

UNICEF. (2003). Trafficking in Human Beings, Especially Women and Children in Africa. UNICEF: Innocenti Research Centre.

UNESCO. (2006). *Human Trafficking in Mozambique. Root Causes and Recommendations* (No.14.1E). United Nations: Educational, Scientific, and Cultural Organization.

U.S. Department of State. (2008, June). *Trafficking in Persons.* Report. Washington, DC: Office to Monitor and Combat Trafficking in Persons.

II

EAST ASIA AND PACIFIC

Kimberly A. McCabe and Sabita Manian

IN CONSIDERING THE DEMOGRAPHIC characteristics of the East Asia and Pacific regions, the diversity of the populations in terms of income, education, and legislative efforts to end human trafficking are apparent. For nearly a decade, the countries of Australia and New Zealand have been classified as Tier 1 countries as they have been in full compliance with the minimum standards of the Trafficking Victims Protection Act, however, the other countries within the region have not demonstrated such a commitment as prevention efforts have essentially been exclusively public awareness campaigns highlighting the dangers in border areas.

Historically, much of the research on sex trafficking has been centered on Asian victims. In fact, many of the early newspaper accounts, case studies, and empirical assessments on sex trafficking depict only Asian women and children as victims. The two chapters in this section—one on China, Thailand, and Vietnam and the other on Taiwan—attempt to provide further details on sex trafficking in these regions as well as discussions of factors which contribute to sex trafficking.

It is acknowledged by these researchers that in countries within East Asia and the Pacific region, sex trafficking is often internal or domestic with the external influences of organized crime and that protection services for victims remain only temporary and inadequate in addressing the needs of victims, especially the child victims, of sex trafficking. It is also acknowledged by these researchers that those involved in the Commercial Sex Trade (CST) have recently incorporated the Internet and chat rooms to identify prospective victims and, similar to U.S. efforts, patrolling the World Wide Web in an attempt to identify human traffickers is simply not financially feasible within the budgets of law enforcement agencies.

In regard to China, as released in the 2006 United Nations report on global patterns in human trafficking, one cannot discount the impact of Chinese organized crime in cases of sex trafficking (UNODC, 2006). The structure of these crime syndicates is well organized with distinct levels of duties and responsibilities and little contact among members. As suggested in discussions on the structure of organized crime in cases of human trafficking, these syndicates are so secretive that identifying and arresting those involved in sex trafficking is a relatively new phenomenon (McCabe, 2008).

Although Thailand became known as a source country for California labor in the 1996 case of the *United States v. Manusurangkun*, it has been identified globally as a source country for sex trafficking. Government officials in Thailand estimate that there are approximately 250,000 sex workers within the country every year. Of course, many of Thailand's victims of sex trafficking are natives of the country; however, many are not. Unfortunately, with immigration laws as they exist within the country, victims of sex trafficking who are not from Thailand often receive nothing in terms of victims' assistance.

The country of Vietnam has received much criticism from American and European authorities on their labor laws and especially those laws regulating exports and the abuse of workers by employers. As related to labor trafficking, Vietnam allows companies to essentially monitor themselves which creates the opportunity for not only national but international abuse. In addition and, as related to this text, Vietnam has also been identified as one of the primary countries for sex trafficking in the United States (McCabe, 2008). As discussed in this section, women and children, anxious to escape the poverty of their native country, leave Vietnam for countries in Europe and Japan and become very easy targets for those interested in obtaining new victims for the sex trade.

During the first few years of the twenty-first century, Taiwan was classified as Tier 1 due to its government efforts to address human trafficking. However, since 2005, law enforcement and nongovernmental organizations in Taiwan have experienced a growth in the number of national and international victims of sex trafficking and has been reclassified as Tier 2. Much of the explanation for Taiwan's decrease in level of tier classification is related to what the United States calls the mail-order bride phenomenon, McCabe's (2007) spousal prostitution, and the use of the Internet in luring victims into the sex trade.

From 2003 to 2007, the U.S. Department of State reports there have been over 7,000 prosecutions for sex trafficking in the East Asia and Pacific region with over 4,500 convictions. In addition, 16 new or amended legislative actions have been enacted to address human trafficking in this geographic region. The two chapters in this section discuss not only the country factors facilitating sex trafficking but also the role of organized crime in cases of human trafficking within the East Asia and Pacific region.

References

McCabe, K. (2007). "Spousal Prostitution." In N. Jackson's *Encyclopedia of Domestic Violence*, pp. 673–674. NY: Routledge.

McCabe, K. (2008). *The Trafficking of Persons: National and International Responses.* NY: Peter Lang.

United Nations Office on Drugs and Crime [UNODC]. (2006, April). *Trafficking in Persons: Global Patterns.* UN: Human Trafficking Unit.

4

An Anatomy of Asian Gangs Involved in Sex Trafficking: An Application of Routine Activities Theory

Nhatthien Q. Nguyen

S EX TRAFFICKING IS HUGELY PROFITABLE and transcends national boundaries. Sex trafficking is the third most profitable criminal activity following only the trafficking of drugs and arms and trafficking victims have been identified in over 150 countries across the globe (Innocenti Research Centre, 2005), with more than 80 percent of trafficking victims being female. China, Thailand, and Vietnam are no exceptions to this rule.

In order to examine the sex trafficking issue, a closer examination of the Routine Activity Theory will give us some clues into the problem. According to the Routine Activity Theory (Curran and Renzetti, 2001), crime results when three factors converge: (1) there are motivated offenders, (2) there are suitable targets, and (3) there is an absence of capable guardians. In this chapter, the *motivated offenders* are the East Asian gangs, the *suitable targets* are the women who are easily recruited by the sex traffickers due to the poor economic conditions of these females, and the *absence of capable guardians* refers to the lack of enforcement against sex traffickers from both sides of the world, the East Asian countries and the West (including North America).

Organized Crime—The Motivated Offenders

An "organized criminal group" is defined as: A structured group of three or more persons existing for a period of time and having the aim of committing a serious crime in order to, directly or indirectly, obtain a financial or other material benefit (Helfand, 2003). The Criminal Intelligence Service of Canada (CISC) observed that Asian gangs not only fit this definition, but also demonstrate "structural fluidity and flexibility" (Helfand, 2003). It is not at all uncommon for members and associates of these groups to conduct numerous dissimilar criminal activities, often with different groups simultaneously, be they ethnically homogeneous or heterogeneous.

As McCabe (2008) suggested, criminal networks involved in human trafficking may be organized in a manner that prohibits an overall knowledge of all the members by each other. In contrast to the Cosa Nostra, which is organized in a pyramid structure making it possible for law enforcement to trace the organization to its highest level, Asian crime groups are organized as autonomous mini-pyramids, with small cells and mini-bosses dictating the actions of only their particular cell. More sophisticated organized crime groups include individuals who engage in frequent travel, both domestically and internationally, often for the purposes of evading law enforcement. Established groups routinely use youth and street gangs not just for their labor but also as a means to expand their activities. The Federal Bureau of Investigation reported that sex trafficking to the United States is controlled by gangs from four East Asian ethnic groups: Chinese, Japanese, Vietnamese and Thai. This chapter will focus on those gangs from China, Thailand, and Vietnam.

Chinese Triads

China has been identified as a source, transit, and destination country for sex trafficking. Since 2001, with the exception of 2007 when China was not ranked, China has been classified as either a Tier 2 or Tier 2 Watch country. Of course, much of China's human trafficking is accomplished through criminal gangs; therefore, detection is extremely difficult. In fact, most, if not all criminal gangs running the sex trafficking industries have their roots in Chinese Triads.

The Triad movement was established in the 1600s with the purpose of overthrowing the Manchu Ching dynasty and restoring the Ming dynasty (Song and Dombrink, 1994). The word "triad" is an English name that describes the triangles indicating the three primary forces of the universe—heaven, earth, and man. Philosophically speaking, the conditions of the heavens and the earth facilitate the success of man. Today, Triads continue to flourish in the United States, Canada, Hong Kong, Malaysia, Singapore, Thailand, Burma, and Taiwan while actively engaging in organized criminal activities.

There is a father-figure in each of the triads to control all other members in illegal activities via a hierarchy (Macko, 1997). Triads are generally composed of several independent groups; however, they work toward a common goal. Although they form and organize themselves with similar hierarchical systems, they do not function under an absolute and strict compliance plan. In fact, group loyalty has lessened in recent years as members might transfer to another group which benefits them personally. Some of the more notorious Chinese Triad gangs include Sun Yee On, 14 K, Big Circle Boys, and Wo On Lok Triads. Four characteristics of Chinese triads have enabled them to avoid detection or penetration of their organization by law enforcement agencies: (1) *International networks*—By using their long cultivated international networks of criminal contacts, the Triads are able to organize and carry out sophisticated transnational criminal activities; (2) *Independence of groups*— Triads operated in loosely independent cells similar to the al-Queda terrorist organization. Organizationally, creation of independent cells minimizes scrutiny of law enforcement. Furthermore, these cells can join forces to conduct business. Upon completion of these projects, they dissolve; (3) *Flexibility and Patience*—Triads will change their method of operation based on each situation. They are also extremely cautious and patient. For example, some sex trafficking victims could be kept at one location for months before the opportunity is right for transporting the victims to their destination; and (4) *Financial Strength*—The Triad criminal project is usually a joint venture that pools the money of several entities together. They also diversify their trades into legitimate businesses, such as restaurants, night clubs, and jewelry stores. Armed with large sums of capital and shielded by their legitimate front companies, they have continued to enrich themselves through their involvement in illegal business ventures with minimum risk (Finckenauer and Chin, 2006). These characteristics ensure that detection by law enforcement is not common and that arrests are rare.

Triads are the primary traffickers of women and girls from Southeast Asia, South America and Eastern Europe to the United States (Macko, 1997). They rely on local brokers who induce women and young girls with job opportunities abroad. Some Triads even resort to kidnapping their victims and transporting them overseas—a phenomenon that happens at a high frequency at the China-Vietnam border. Upon arrival, the victims are held prisoner until further money is paid. Noteworthy is China's recent efforts to (a) build shelters for trafficking victims such as the one in the Yunnan Province; and (b) implement efforts to identify trafficking victims through cross-border agency cooperation. However, little in terms of evaluation/assessment exists on the impact of those shelters on the criminal activity of sex trafficking.

Thai Criminal Networks

Thailand has been identified as a source, transit, and destination country for sex trafficking. Since 2001, the country has been classified as either a Tier 2 or

Tier 2 Watch country. The leading organized crime group in Thailand is the *Jao Pho* or Godfather (Finckenauer and Chin, 2006). Since the 1960s, the rapid pace of industrialization and urban growth in Thailand created a power vacuum in many areas where lawlessness was the rule. *Jao Pho*, which is comprised of provincial businessmen and their underlings, stepped in to fill the "power vacuum" in establishing law and order. As the political process and the military restored law and order, *Jao Pho* turned their functions to profit making opportunities which include sex trafficking (Phongpaichit, 2004) and this continues to flourish to this day.

Jao Pho is comprised of mostly ethnic-Chinese based in the provinces who have business interests in both legitimate and criminal activities. They operate independently even though their methods of operation are similar: maximizing profit by any means and establishing connections with important government officials. Invariably, they are allied with powerful bureaucrats, policemen and military figures through bribery and "*under the table*" dealings (Phongpaichit, 2004). As suggested by research in criminal justice, without concentrated efforts by law enforcement to reduce sex trafficking, the activity continues.

Prostitution is vital to Thailand's enormous tourist industry and corrupt government officials aid the *Jao Pho* groups' capabilities to import women in Southeast Asia, particularly from Burma to Thailand and then into the United States. Because of their extensive network, *Jao Pho* groups not only traffic the women and children, they also operate the brothels, thus maintaining control over the entire operation. To avoid detection by law enforcement officials, these women, especially in the United States, are rotated to different locations every few weeks/months. However, it must be acknowledged that Thai officials are pursuing efforts to reduce sex trafficking as Thai law enforcement and prosecutors reported the arrest and prosecution of approximately 150 sex trafficking cases between July 2005 and June 2007. Additionally, government authorities continue with awareness programs on the illegal sex tourism industry.

The Vietnamese Gangs

Vietnam has been identified as a source, transit, and destination country for sex trafficking. Since 2002, Vietnam has been classified as either a Tier 2 or Tier 2 Watch country. The fall of Saigon in 1975, which officially ended the Vietnam War, brought a great influx of Vietnamese refugees to the United States. Invariably, the remnants of the gangs from Vietnam also made their way to the United States. Faced with a different culture and language, coupled with conflicting values from their families and society, many Vietnamese youths in the United States joined gangs to gain acceptance and promises of money, drugs and sex (Long, 1997). Although lacking the operational sophistication when compared to the Chinese Triads, Vietnamese gangs are notorious for their ruthlessness in intimidating their victims.

In contrast to the Chinese Triad, there are no dominant gangs either in Vietnam or in the United States. However, these gangs in general, share certain characteristics. First, they are highly mobile in order to evade authorities. As a matter of fact, they usually set up a "safe house" in each area that they travel to (Long, 1997). Second, they have no hesitation in sending out messages that they mean business through brutal killings such as slitting the throats of their victims and leaving these victims in plain sight to assure discovery and an audience. It should be noted that some groups, such as the New York–based BTK (Born to Kill) gang, are well structured with a definite leadership hierarchy while most other gangs are quite unstructured with constantly changing affiliation.

Vietnam has an extremely high level of poverty therefore Vietnamese gangs can easily entice women from poor areas to apply for work overseas, making false promises of jobs as waitresses, nannies, models, and factory workers with high wages and good working conditions (Richard, 2000). Recruiters front the money for travel documents, transportation, and charge the women or children from $25,000 to $30,000 for their services. Once recruited, the women's passports are confiscated, their movements are restricted, and many are forced to work as prostitutes until their debts are repaid. Women are prevented from leaving through violence, or threats of violence to themselves or their families. Trafficking victims may also suffer from extreme physical and mental abuse, including rape, imprisonment, and forced abortions. Vietnamese gangs more often act as "muscle" for other more organized gangs such as the Chinese Triads in recruiting or kidnapping women and/or children and transport them to a "safe house" in another country before being transported to the United States. It must be noted that centers to support victims have been established in localities such as Hanoi and aggressive public awareness campaigns attempt to educate all the residents on the evils of sex trafficking. However, no evaluation/assessment as yet exists on the utility of these shelters.

Victims—The Suitable Targets

Sex trafficking is a regrettably widespread form of modern-day slavery (Gonzales, 2006). An estimated 600,000 to 800,000 human beings are trafficked across international borders each year. More than 80 percent of these victims are women and girls, and 70 percent of them are forced into sexual servitude. Furthermore, one estimate claims that between 14,500 and 17,500 victims may be trafficked into the United States each year. Unfortunately, in East Asia, because the rate of poverty is so much higher, young girls as young as five are sold into sexual slavery or exported to industrialized countries such as the United States where the sex industry is booming.

Several legal barriers exists which provide support for sex trafficking. Specifically, since sex trafficking is often closely associated with organized crime, trafficking victims generally do not seek out local authorities for help for fear of retaliation against themselves and their families. Also, due to their lack of understanding of the American legal system, trafficking victims are reluctant to cooperate with law enforcement authorities for fear of deportation and prosecution. In addition, most victims of sex trafficking are distrustful of U.S. authority figures because of known corruption in their home countries. Finally, traffickers often move their victims every 15 to 30 days and limit their victims' contact with the outside world; thus, victims generally are unable to develop outside social networks in order to escape.

Lack of Capable Guardians—Perceptions of Law Enforcement Officers

Sex trafficking is not recognized as a serious problem in many Asian countries for three main reasons: First, corruption is a leading factor in the sex trafficking trade. Organized crime, through their huge profits, is able to ally themselves with top government officials in forging documents, facilitating the passport process and avoiding detection from authorities. Second, in some countries, especially Thailand, sex trafficking is encouraged to satisfy the demands of the sex tourism industry which for the national government is a large portion of its total revenues. In fact, Thailand recently proposed to establish prostitution zones similar to Australia's Victoria prostitution areas. Third, sex trafficking is not recognized as a normal crime, such as murder or robbery; thus, police efforts are not utilized to target or reduce sex trafficking. Finally, in many Asian cultures, there is a relative normative acceptance of the concept of human servitude, particularly the servitude of children, women and the poor (Iselin, 2002).

Conclusion

Sex trafficking is a global phenomenon that does not recognize national borders. Realizing the serious consequence on the human toll, in 2002, the U.S. government spent $55 million in 50 countries on anti-trafficking programs. These programs are designed to help indigenous nongovernmental organizations (NGOs), international organizations, law enforcement officials, and foreign governments prevent human trafficking, and restore victims to society. By educating the public about the various programs designed to protect the victims such as the Trafficking Victims Protection Act of 2000, innocent victims are more likely to step forward.

The three major Asian gangs discussed in this chapter share a common tactic in transferring their victims—they have found ways to exploit the "holes" in U.S. immigration law to send their victims to the United States. For example, foreign women and children can enter the United States legally as students, visitors, domestic workers, or mail-order brides. Furthermore, responsibilities such as recruitment, document forgery, transportation, and employment are subcontracted out. For example, a woman in one of the countries typically involved in trafficking may respond to an advertisement for a seemingly legitimate job, only to be deceived into agreeing to be transported to the United States. Sex traffickers routinely make use of the Chinese smuggling network, known as "snakeheads," which often moves aliens into the United States in maritime vessels. Some gangs charge their victims as much as $40,000 for passage to the United States. Consequently, many of their victims are enslaved as sex workers for years before being released, if they are lucky. This enormous problem can be explained by the Routine Activity Theory with its three main components: Motivated Offenders, represented by a hugely profitable market of sex trafficking run by the Asian gangs; Suitable Targets, the easily misled women from the economically depressed regions of the world; and the Lack of Capable Guardians, the "don't care" attitude from both the East Asian countries and the United States' law enforcement agencies. Although each Asian gang's structure and method of recruiting their victims may vary, the methods of transferring their victims to the United States are similar. In sum, the involvement of Asian organized crimes in sex trafficking poses a special challenge to U.S. law enforcement efforts.

References

Assessment of U.S. Activities to Combat Trafficking in Persons. (2003). Washington, DC: U.S. Department of Justice, National Institute of Justice.

Clawson, H. J., Dutch, N., and Cummings, M. (2006). *Law Enforcement Response to Human Trafficking and the Implications for Victims: Current Practices and Lesson Learned.* Washington, DC: U.S. Department of Justice, National Institute of Justice.

Curran, D.J., and Renzetti, C.M. (2001). *Theories of Crime* (2nd ed.). Boston: Allyn and Bacon.

Finckenauer, J. O., and Chin, K. (2006). *Asian Transnational Organized Crime and Its Impact on the United States: Developing a Transnational Crime Research Agenda.* Washington, DC: U.S. Department of Justice, National Institute of Justice.

Gonzales, A. (2006). *Attorney General's Annual Report to Congress on U.S. Government Activities to Combat Trafficking in Persons Fiscal Year 2005.* Washington, DC: Federal Research Division, Library of Congress.

Helfand, N. S. (2003). *Asian Organized Crime and Terrorist Activity in Canada, 1999–2002.*

Innocenti Research Centre (2005). *Trafficking for Sexual Exploitation Purposes.* United Nations Children's Fund. www. Unicef-icdc.org/publications/pdf/trafficking-exploitation-eng.pdf.

Iselin, B. (2002). *Barriers to Effective Human Trafficking Enforcement in the Mekong Sub-Region.* United Nations' Office on Drugs and Crime.

Long, P. (with Richard, L.) (1997). *The Dream Shattered: Vietnamese Gangs in America.* Boston: Northeastern University Press.

Macko, S. (1997). *Chinese Triads; an Update.* Emergency Services Report: Chicago, Illinois.

Marshall, P., and Thatun, S. (1998). *Training Manual for Combating Trafficking in Women and Children.* UN–Interagency Project on Combating Trafficking in Women and Children in the Sub-Mekong Region.

May, M. (2006, October 8). A Youthful Mistake. *San Francisco Chronicle,* p. 2.

McCabe, K. (2008). *The Trafficking of Persons: National and International Responses.* NY: Peter Lang.

Osborne, D. (2006). *Out of Bounds: Innovation in Law Enforcement Intelligence Analysis.* Washington, DC: Joint Military Intelligence College.

Peterson, M. (2005). *Intelligence-Led Policing: the New Intelligence Architecture.* Washington, DC: Bureau of Justice Assistance.

Phongpaichit, P. (2004). *Thailand under Thaksin: Another Malaysia?* National Library of Australia: Working Paper No. 109.

Richard, A. O. (2000). *International Trafficking in Women to the United States: A Contemporary Manifestation of Slavery and Organized Crime.* State Department's Bureau of Intelligence and Research.

Song, J., and Dombrink, J. (1994). *Asian Emerging Crime Groups: Examining the Definition of Organized Crime.* Criminal Justice Review, 19(2).

5

Taiwan's Efforts to Combat Human Trafficking between 2001 and 2008

Yingyu Chen

TAIWAN IS AN ISLAND COUNTRY located between Japan and the Philippines in the western Pacific while the Taiwan Strait separates Taiwan from the People's Republic of China. Its geostrategic location creates a transportation hub for Northeast and Southeast Asia, which facilitates trade and commerce. The 1980s economic boom in East Asia created a demand for cheap laborers from Southeast Asia, particularly in the areas of manufacturing and construction (Skolnik and Boontinand, 1999). Furthermore, globalization and industrialization in the past decade have transformed the traditional local or regional businesses into global ones, increasing the flows of goods, finance, and people. Taiwan's economic growth with globalization has led to a rise in migrant workers.

The intra- and transnational labor migration has become one of the livelihood options for people from poor countries; where the migration is for survival rather than opportunity seeking (Chuang, 2006). However, with the increase of immigrants and migrant workers, host countries have tougher border control and more restrictive immigration policies in the name of homeland security and/or of easing the growing resistance to new arrivals (Tomasi, 2000). These measures have fostered the emergence of illegal migration including smuggling and trafficking in persons. In Asia, most human trafficking cases are intra-regional—victims are trafficked from one Asian country to another. Taiwan has been frequently reported as one of the destination countries in Asia, and trafficking victims are mainly from India, the Philippines, and Vietnam (United Nations Office on Drugs and Crime, 2006).

Skolnik and Boontinand note that in many Asian countries, due to political, cultural, or socioeconomic factors, more women than men leave their countries looking for work and better wages (1999). However, employment opportunities for women migrant workers are limited to low-paying and low-skilled jobs, such as domestic helper, caretaker, factory or restaurant worker, or entertainers. These women often do not have sufficient information to understand the legal channels regarding job-seeking and easily fall prey to traffickers. Traffickers often target poor and vulnerable families, or use local villagers to find young women (Flamm, 2003). Women are frequently dependent on the arrangements made by other people, especially by brokers or matchmakers, who may use coercive or deceptive measures to bring them into Taiwan through either legal or illegal channels. Contrary to the popular thought that women are forced or kidnapped to leave their countries, they often make decisions by themselves (Chuang, 2006). However, their decisions are based on false and misleading information offered by traffickers.

Women are trafficked into Taiwan for the purposes of sexual exploitation, involuntary servitude, or forced labor, but they may not have the same resources once they are identified as victims of human trafficking. Chen (2008) found that women who entered Taiwan on work visas but were then exploited were more likely to have access to legal remedies than those who entered Taiwan on fake marriages or tourist visas. Chen interviewed 81 female victims of trafficking in Taiwan between 2007 and 2008 and noted seven patterns of human trafficking in Taiwan by examining methods of entry and subsequent exploitation of trafficked victims. The first two means included the traffickers' use of work visas and fraudulent marriages. All the women surveyed wanted to make more money to overcome financial hardship or pursue better living standards for their families. They were recruited in their home countries by brokers referred by family-friends, neighbors, or newspaper advertisements, and were promised domestic, manufacturing, or entertainment jobs. However, once in Taiwan, they found themselves in exploitative work situations: receive no salaries or only partial salaries, and/or engage in work exceeding ten hours per day without break, or work they had not signed on to doing, while their passports or other important documents (e.g., Alien Resident Certificate) were confiscated by the brokers or employers.

Women who came to Taiwan using fake marriages or tourist visas were more vulnerable and might be subjected to further exploitation because of their illegal immigration status. Furthermore, these women were likely to develop strong bonds with their traffickers because they had cultural and language barriers, and were not protected by Taiwan's Labor Standards Law. Lack of resources to seek help prevented them from escaping the exploitative situation. Under these circumstances, these women were trapped in a relationship that might not easily be severed. If they file any complaints against their employers (or traffickers) or report the crime to the police, there is a good chance that they may be arrested as illegal migrants, instead of being treated as victims of human trafficking. The rapid growth of human trafficking has caused Taiwan's drop in Tier rankings in the Trafficking in Persons (TIP) Reports.

Taiwan's Tier Rankings

2001–2004: Tier 1

According to the 2001, 2003, and 2004 TIP Report, Taiwan was placed in Tier 1 from 2001 to 2004 (and not ranked in 2002), and Taiwan was identified as a source, transit, and destination country for people trafficked for the purposes of sexual exploitation and forced labor. Victims were mainly from the People's Republic of China (P.R.C.) and Southeast Asian countries such as Cambodia, Indonesia, Thailand, and Vietnam. Some women were lured into Taiwan by fraudulent employment opportunities while some women came by fake marriages to Taiwanese men. Taiwanese women were trafficked to Japan for commercial sexual exploitation (CSE). Taiwan was also a transit point for illegal migrants who were trafficked to North America. These same TIP reports also indicated that Taiwan's law enforcement officials received training to investigate and prosecute cases of human trafficking. Although Taiwan did not have a specific anti-trafficking law, provisions of other laws, for examples, the Criminal Law and the Law to Suppress Sexual Transactions Involving Children and Juveniles, were applied to trafficking-related crime. The government also worked closely with NGOs and provided services to both child and adult victims of human trafficking, including temporary housing/shelter, medical assistance, legal aid, and counseling.

2005: Tier 2

The 2005 TIP Report indicated that Taiwan did not fully comply with the minimum standards for the elimination of trafficking, but was making significant efforts to do so. Taiwan was a source and a destination country for victims from the P.R.C., Thailand, Cambodia, and Vietnam. Luring victims into coming to Taiwan by fraudulent job offers or marriages, the traffickers coerced them into prostitution (TIP Report, 2005).

Although Taiwan had other laws (e.g., Articles 296 and 296–1 of the Criminal Law) to prosecute cases of human trafficking, Taiwan did not have a comprehensive anti-trafficking law to protect victims and to provide for prevention activities. The law enforcement officials sometimes could not distinguish between trafficking and smuggling, and therefore victims were not properly identified and were placed in detention centers. Furthermore, victims from P.R.C. were not as quickly repatriated as victims from other countries, and no legal alternatives to repatriation were provided to trafficking victims. The government continued to collaborate with NGOs to raise public awareness of sex trafficking of minors and Southeast Asian women who married Taiwanese men (TIP, 2005).

2006: Tier 2 Watch List

In 2006, Taiwan fell to Tier 2 Watch List because the government failed to provide evidence of increasing efforts over the previous year to fight against forced labor and sex trade, such as the lack of comprehensive anti-trafficking law to prosecute all forms of trafficking in persons, particularly forced labor, and insufficient protection for trafficked victims (TIP, 2006). The traffickers who were found guilty of exploiting foreign workers only received administrative fines (TIP, 2006). Additionally, the recruitment procedures for foreign laborers and brides was not adequately monitored, since many were subjected to sex work, forced labor, or involuntary servitude by traffickers. Approximately 6 percent of the migrant workers left their work because of abuse or intolerable working conditions, but were treated as law-breakers by law enforcement agencies; these "runaways" often became victims of sex trade or forced labor (TIP Report, 2006). There were no shelters specifically designed for victims of human trafficking, and no alternatives to repatriation were offered to victims (TIP Report, 2006).

2007: Tier 2

Taiwan returned to Tier 2 in 2007 and as in previous years, Taiwan continued to be a destination country for sex and labor trafficking, with victims mainly from the P.R.C. and Southeast Asia (TIP Report, 2007). Although Taipei developed the National Action Plan to show its commitment to combat trafficking in persons, Taiwan still lacked a comprehensive anti-trafficking law to criminalize all forms of trafficking and its related acts, particularly debt bondage and other forms of labor exploitation. The Council of Labor Affairs (CLA) often treated exploitative work situations as labor disputes without referring exploited migrant workers to the law enforcement officials for further criminal investigation (TIP Report, 2007).

2008: Tier 2

According to the 2008 TIP Report, Taiwan remained a destination country for sexual exploitation and forced labor, and was also a source country in which women were trafficked to Japan, Australia, the United Kingdom, and the United States. An increasing number of boys were sexually exploited through online social networking sites (TIP, 2008). The 2008 TIP Report suggests that Taiwan is in need of a comprehensive anti-trafficking law because punishments imposed on traffickers convicted of sexual or labor exploitation under the existing laws are too lenient. Even though Taipei had allocated a budget to design shelters specifically for trafficking victims to provide better services, the 2008 TIP Report noted that large numbers of trafficking victims were not identified as such; instead, they were categorized as illegal immigrants or workers and placed in overcrowded detention facilities (TIP Report, 2008).

Since it is not recognized as a nation-state and it lacks diplomatic relationship with many of the origin countries, Taiwan is limited in its efforts to reduce human trafficking.

Tier Rankings and Taiwan's Efforts

Fewer actions were specifically designed to fight trafficking in persons when Taiwan was ranked Tier 1 between 2001 and 2004. In August 2005, the amendments to the Immigration Law, which focused on prevention of human trafficking and victim protection, were sent to the Legislative Yuan, for review (The Ministry of the Interior, 2007). Meanwhile, the Ministry of Justice collaborated with Taipei Women's Rescue Foundation to hold an international training workshop on prevention of human trafficking in May 2005, and added human trafficking issues into the annual in-service training for prosecutors (The Ministry of Justice, 2006). Taiwan, however, had not taken major steps to combat trafficking in persons until 2006 when Taiwan was placed on Tier 2 Watch List in the TIP Report. The 2006 TIP Report stated that Taiwan failed to "address the serious level of forced labor and sexual servitude among legally migrating Southeast Asian contract workers and brides," criticizing the lack of an anti-trafficking law and inadequate protection for victims of trafficking (238).

In response to the drop in the tier ranking, the Executive Yuan convened eight interagency meetings and consulted with scholars to draft the National Action Plan (NAP) for Combating Trafficking in Persons, which was promulgated in November 2006 (The Executive Yuan, 2007). In accordance with the

United Nations *Protocol to Prevent, Suppress and Punish Trafficking in Persons, Especially Women and Children, Supplementing the United Nations Convention against Transnational Organized Crime* in 2000, the NAP emphasizes three strategic elements: prevention, prosecution, and protection. The NAP primarily aims to protect victims' human rights, followed by crime investigation, criminal prosecution, awareness-raising campaigns, and international collaboration in order to establish a comprehensive anti-trafficking approach (The Executive Yuan, 2006).

Additionally, the Executive Yuan established the Administrative Council Meeting on Prevention of Human Trafficking, which has been regularly convened once every two months since March 2007, to provide a communication platform for governmental agencies and NGOs to discuss issues related to human trafficking. Each governmental agency and NGO has assigned a point of contact to facilitate communication and coordination between organizations (The Executive Yuan, 2007). The Ministry of Justice developed an Executive Plan for Prevention of Human Trafficking Cases on December 12, 2006, mandating every district court to appoint prosecutors specializing in human trafficking cases: the Taiwan High Court had to form a supervision unit, and the Prosecutors Office for the Taiwan High Court is to organize all human trafficking cases (The Executive Yuan). Aside from improving coordination and cooperation between the governmental and nongovernmental organizations, between March 2006–2007, the government organized (a) several awareness-raising campaigns targeting foreign spouses, migrant workers and the general public, (b) alleviated change of employer restrictions imposed on migrant workers, (c) increased collaboration with foreign countries and the international organizations, (d) intensified investigation into human trafficking cases, and (e) developed better screening of trafficking victims (The Executive Yuan).

Taiwan reverted to Tier 2 in 2007 because of the aforementioned efforts between 2006 and 2007. The 2007 TIP Report, however, pointed out that the Taiwan government still provided inadequate assistance and protection for victims, and the punishment imposed on traffickers was too lenient (TIP Report, 2007). As a result, the Taiwan government's efforts between 2007 and 2008 focused more on victim protection and drafting the first anti-trafficking legislation. The Ministry of Justice developed formal procedures, intending to help law enforcement officers proactively identify more victims of human trafficking (The Executive Yuan, 2008). Once a victim is identified, the law enforcement agency follows the official protocol to provide appropriate shelters or housing and other related assistance, for example, financial assistance as deemed necessary (The Executive Yuan). The Ministry of Justice also collaborates with the Association for Protection of Victims of Criminal Acts

(APVCA) to provide care for the victims, including informing their families in the countries of origin and embassies in Taipei of their physical safety (The Executive Yuan).

Moreover, the government has established several mechanisms to protect victims during investigation and prosecution. One mechanism requires social workers to accompany victims during questioning by law enforcement personnel since December 2006, and in November 2007 the Ministry of the Interior established an official protocol to ensure victims' physical safety when they go to court to testify (The Executive Yuan, 2008). The Ministry of the Interior, along with the Council of Labor Affairs (CLA), built a database of interpreters in each local government to provide interpretation services for trafficking victims; the Ministry of the Interior also developed repatriation regulation in January 2008 to safely return victims to their countries of origin (The Executive Yuan). The government also relaxed foreign labor policies in an attempt to reduce illegal migrant workers: they created a Direct Employment Center in December 2007 to make hiring process more efficient, eased restrictions on change of employers, and improved protection for migrant workers' rights (The Executive Yuan).

In addition to victim protection and re-examination of foreign labor policies, the government passed amendments to the Immigration Law on December 26, 2007, which added chapter 7 to regulate protection for trafficking victims and witnesses (The Executive Yuan, 2008). The Taipei government also drafted an anti-trafficking law to supplement the Criminal Law, to build a victim protection network, and to enhance service providers' knowledge about human trafficking (The Executive Yuan). Furthermore, the Taiwan government, between March 2007 and March 2008, continued to provide training for law enforcement personnel and other service providers, hold awareness-raising campaigns, collaborate with NGOs, investigate suspected human trafficking cases, and improve international coordination. Despite these efforts, Taiwan remained Tier 2 in the 2008 TIP Report (TIP Report, 2008).

Conclusion

Taiwan had been placed on Tier 1 from 2001 to 2004 in the TIP Reports, even without Taipei having taken significant actions against trafficking in persons. The government started to take major steps to combat the crime when Taiwan fell to Tier 2 Watch List in the 2006 TIP Report. Taiwan subsequently developed the first National Action Plan and took measures to combat human trafficking by coordinating a communication platform for governmental agencies and nongovernmental organizations. These efforts helped Taiwan return to Tier 2, but the 2007 TIP Report still criticized the government's inadequate victim protection as well as lack of a comprehensive anti-trafficking law. In response to the criticism, the government improved victim and witness protection and drafted the first anti-trafficking law. Taiwan remained Tier 2 in the 2008 TIP Report. Currently, the government continues to collaborate with NGOs to provide better services to victims, and attempts to reach a consensus with the Coalition against Human Trafficking (a network of NGOs) on the scope of anti-trafficking legislation. The controversial political status of Taiwan has made it difficult to establish diplomatic relations with other foreign countries, which has formed a big obstacle to the prevention of this transnational crime.

References

Chen, Y. (2008). *Patterns of human trafficking and assessment of victim services needs in Taiwan: Final research report* (in Chinese). Taipei, Taiwan: Taipei Women's Rescue Foundation.

Chuang, J. (2006). Beyond a snapshot: Preventing human trafficking in the global economy. *Indiana Journal of Global Legal Studies*, 13, 137–163.

Flamm, M. (2003). Trafficking of women and children in Southeast Asia. *UN Chronicle*, 40, 34–36.

Skolnik, L., and Boontinand, J. (1999). Traffic in women in Asia-Pacific. *Forum for Applied Research and Public Policy*, 14, 76–81.

The Executive Yuan (2006). *The National Action Plan for Combating Trafficking in Persons.* Taipei: The Executive Yuan.

———. (2007). *2006 Report on prevention of trafficking in persons.* Taipei: The Executive Yuan.

———. (2008). *2007 Report on prevention of trafficking in persons.* Taipei: The Executive Yuan.

The Ministry of Justice. (2006). *The current situations of human trafficking cases.* <http://www.moj.gov.tw/ct.asp?xItem=39019&ctNode=13840&mp=001> (5 Jan. 2009).

The Ministry of the Interior. (2007). *The Legislative Yuan passed the Amendments to the Immigration Law today (11/30).* <ww.moi.gov.tw/news_history_detail.aspx?sn=544> (5 Jan. 2009).

Tomasi, L. F. (2000). Globalization and human trafficking. *Migration World Magazine*, 28, 4.

Trafficking Victims Protection Act of 2000 § 108, 22 U.S.C. § 7106 (2000).

Trafficking Victims Protection Act of 2000 § 110, 22 U.S.C. § 7107 (2000) (amended 2003).

United Nations Office on Drugs and Crime. (2006). *Trafficking in persons: Global patterns.* Vienna, Austria: UNDOC. <http://www.unodc.org/pdf/traffickinginpersons_report_2006-04.pdf> (5 Jan. 2009).

U.S. Department of State. (2001, July). *Trafficking in Persons*. Report. Washington, DC: Office to Monitor and Combat Trafficking in Persons.

U.S. Department of State. (2003, July). *Trafficking in Persons*. Report. Washington, DC: Office to Monitor and Combat Trafficking in Persons.

U.S. Department of State. (2004, July). *Trafficking in Persons*. Report. Washington, DC: Office to Monitor and Combat Trafficking in Persons.

U.S. Department of State. (2005, July). *Trafficking in Persons*. Report. Washington, DC: Office to Monitor and Combat Trafficking in Persons.

U.S. Department of State. (2006, July). *Trafficking in Persons*. Report. Washington, DC: Office to Monitor and Combat Trafficking in Persons.

U.S. Department of State. (2007, July). *Trafficking in Persons*. Report. Washington, DC: Office to Monitor and Combat Trafficking in Persons.

U.S. Department of State. (2008, July). *Trafficking in Persons*. Report. Washington, DC: Office to Monitor and Combat Trafficking in Persons.

III

EUROPE

Kimberly A. McCabe and Sabita Manian

E UROPE, AT THE END OF THE TWENTIETH century and today, has experienced very low birth rates and, with the exception of the United Kingdom and perhaps one or two other countries, the only increase in population is a result of immigration. Of course, in countries that have steady flows of immigrants, there is an expectation of nonnative inhabitants; thus, individuals trafficked into a country for the purpose of sexual exploitation may exist within the country without question. Of the 29 countries classified as Tier 1 in the 2008 Trafficking in Persons Report, the majority are in Europe. The two chapters in this section on Europe—one on the United Kingdom and the other on the countries of Austria, Poland, and Croatia—attempt to identify strengths and weaknesses in terms of their efforts to reduce sex trafficking.

The United Kingdom (UK) has been identified as primarily a destination country for human trafficking for victims from countries such as Russia, Thailand, and Africa (McCabe, 2008). Of course, anyone who has traveled to other countries in Western Europe has probably transitioned through London, hence the UK may also serve as a major transit country for men, women, and children being trafficked to other destination countries for sexual victimization. As discussed in this section, the UK is a country with often internal procedural conflicts between immigration legislation and laws and policies to protect victims of sexual exploitation and sex trafficking. In addition, UK legal distinctions between smuggling and trafficking are not as clear as legislative efforts have suggested (ECPAT, 2007) and therefore law enforcement efforts have not been as successful.

Austria, a country often viewed as a stopover country for those Americans visiting Germany, has been one of the leaders in the European Union in terms of human trafficking treaties and legislation. In fact, after noting the problems of clear definitions and comparable data collections, Austrian officials have initiated projects for data collection within the European Union. In addition, Austria is often identified as a model country because of its treatment of victims of sex trafficking. In Austria, if the victim chooses to return to their native country, the government arranges the transportation. If the victim chooses to remain within the country, the Austrian government provides temporary visa.

The overwhelming majority of the victims of human trafficking in Poland are victims of sex trafficking. Many of the victims within Poland are from Russia and travel through Poland en route to other destination countries (McCabe, 2008). Polish authorities have been very aggressive in their pursuits of traffickers as human trafficking is punishable as forced prostitution and/or trafficking. In addition, the Polish government has been applauded for its cooperative efforts with other countries such as Germany, Italy, and the Ukraine on trafficking cases and the relocation of victims.

Of all the European countries highlighted in this section, Croatia is the least progressive in terms of its efforts to reduce sex trafficking. Croatia is considered an affluent country relative to many of the other countries within the region, therefore it is often a destination country for victims of sex trafficking (Limanowska, 2005). The country has been recently classified as a Tier 1 country as the government implemented migration policies which incorporate procedures for addressing cases of sex trafficking. However, it is acknowledged that Croatia's ability to identify victims of sex trafficking has been limited over the years and just recently as specific anti-trafficking training been introduced to Croatia's law enforcement officers.

From 2003 to 2007, Europe surpasses all other geographic regions in its legal initiatives to end human trafficking. Specifically, Europe averages approximately 2,700 prosecutions for sex trafficking on an annual basis with approximately 1,600 convictions. In addition, from 2003 to 2007, sixty new or amended legislative actions have been adopted as measures to reduce human trafficking. The two chapters in this section, discuss not only the successful practices of the countries in terms of efforts to reduce sex trafficking but also specific areas in need of further attention. Significant to this section and the two chapters within this section is the generalization that even countries with the best tier classifications are still attempting to refine current practices and in search of new methods to end sex trafficking.

References

ECPAT (2007). *Missing Out. A Study of Child Trafficking in the Northwest, Northeast, and West Midlands.* London, England: ECPAT.

Limanowska, B. (2005). *Trafficking in Human Beings in South Eastern Europe.* <http://www.osce.org/publications/odihr/2005/04/13771_211_en.pdf> (3 Sept. 2009).

McCabe, K. (2008). *The Trafficking of Persons: National and International Responses.* NY: Peter Lang.

6

Mercenary Territory:
A UK Perspective on Human Trafficking

Margaret Melrose

THIS CHAPTER PROVIDES A DISCUSSION of the phenomenon of human trafficking from the perspective of the UK. It considers the location of the UK as a source, transit or destination country, the position of the UK in the United States government's tier ranking of other countries' measures to combat human trafficking and discusses initiatives pursued by the UK government to combat human trafficking.

The chapter contends that the approach toward human trafficking adopted by the British government is situated within its wider concern to manage immigration. As such its interest is primarily focused on organized crime and border control rather than with the abuses of human rights that processes of human trafficking inevitably entail (Refugee Council, 2006; Women's Commission, 2005). This results in a conflict between tackling organized crime and controlling migratory processes on the one hand and victim protection on the other.

Constructing the Problem of Trafficking

It is only relatively recently that an international definition of human trafficking has been agreed. This chapter will follow the definition of the Palermo Protocol, UN 2000 (see introduction). Whether a person is considered to be "trafficked" or "smuggled" makes an important difference in terms of the rights they may receive upon arrival in the UK and consequently their treatment in this country.

End Child Prostitution and Trafficking (ECPAT, 2007, 12) contend that it is "essential" that practitioners do not confuse these processes "in order to ensure that children are provided with the most appropriate care and legal support". However, these processes are frequently confused or conflated (Iselin and Adams, 2003; Andrijasevic, 2003; Experts Group on Trafficking in Human Beings, 2004). This may be because, as Kelly (2007) and others suggest, these two processes are not necessarily as distinct as legal definitions would suggest (q.v. Hudson, 2007; Lee, 2007). The distinction between "human trafficking" and "human smuggling" tends to construct the former as "victims" of crimes committed against them and the latter as complicit in crimes committed against the state (i.e., the violation of immigration law) (Hudson, 2007; Lee, 2007; Carling, 2006). Generally it is women and young people who are trafficked and men who are smuggled (Gallagher, 2001; Kangaspunta, 2003; Morrison, 2004; Monzini, 2005; Melrose and Barrett, 2006; Nieuwenhuys and Pecoud, 2007; Lee, 2007). Thus the former tend to be constructed as "victims" and the latter as complicit in crimes against the state.

It is possible, however, that because these processes are not as distinct as the law constructs them to be that a "smuggled" person may find themselves in "bonded labor situations when they arrive at their destinations" (Hudson, 2007, 212). A trafficked person on the other hand may have embarked voluntarily on their journey but instead of the well-paid, glamorous job they were expecting, find themselves working in conditions, or indeed in an illicit or illegal sector of the labor market, that they had not anticipated (Brown, 2000; Andrijasevic, 2003; Carling, 2006; Hudson, 2007). "Smuggling" and "trafficking" are therefore better understood as a continuum of predatory and exploitative practices. These practices involve not only physical and/or sexual exploitation but also exploitation of the hopes, dreams and desires of people wishing to escape torture, conflict and/or poverty in their country of origin (Moorehead, 2006). The UN trafficking protocol states that consent is irrelevant if a person has been tricked, coerced or threatened yet the UK continues to use this distinction in its response to victims of trafficking (Women's Commission, 2005). This is because these categories are political constructions through which the British government endeavors to control immigration. They are treated, however, as if they were "reflections of real differences in the motivations and circumstances of migrants" (Hudson, 2007, 211).

Human trafficking occurs for a variety of purposes including labor exploitation and domestic servitude, forced marriage, use of body parts and for the purpose of commercial sexual exploitation (CSE) (Lee, 2007; Kapoor, 2007; Melrose and Barrett, 2006). In Britain, the focus until relatively recently has been primarily on trafficking for the purpose of CSE.

Human trafficking is constructed as a different sort of problem by a variety of social actors, agencies and institutions (O'Connell-Davidson, 2002). NGOs tend to construct it as a problem of human rights abuses (Mecham, 2006) while government agencies such as the police and the immigration service construct it either as a problem of organized crime, or as a problem of illegal immigration on the other (Kelly and Regan, 2000; Taylor, 2005). Understandings of how the problem should be confronted therefore, vary according to the discourse that constructs the problem (Refugee Council, 2006; Taylor, 2005; Kelly and Regan, 2000).

Source, Transit, and Destination Countries

Human trafficking networks are characterized by some elements of the network being more loosely connected than others (Salt, 2000). There is no uniformity within and between these networks (O'Connell-Davidson and Donelan, 2003 cited in Laczko and Gramegna, 2003) although most are to some degree or another hierarchically organized (Salt, 2000). Networks organizing the trafficking of people over long distances are likely to be more highly organized than those organizing them over shorter distances (Futo et al., 2005).

Trafficking routes are complex but adaptable and can change quickly and easily when necessary (Salt, 2000). The value of distinguishing between "source," "transit," and "destination" countries has therefore been called into question as it is clear that some countries act as all three (Lehti, 2003). Present evidence suggests that the UK is both an area of destination and an area of transit for women and young people who are trafficked (ECPAT, 2007). Women from many parts of the world have been working in the UK sex industry; the majority of these come from Eastern Europe, China and South East Asia, Africa and Brazil. (Dickson, 2004).

Foreign Women in the UK Sex Industry

In 2003 a survey of sex work establishments across London's 33 boroughs identified 894 sex work premises (including saunas, massage parlors, flats and escort agencies). Approximately 80 percent of women working in these establishments were identified as non-UK nationals with the largest ethnic group being Eastern European. The study estimated there were between 4727 and 8082 women working in these premises. Most of these women were aged between 18 and 28 years. Some had been trafficked for sex work while others had migrated. The study found it was very rare for women who had been trafficked into the

UK to be involved in street prostitution (Dickson, 2004). The findings from this survey correspond with evidence produced from national policing operations (involving all 55 police forces) to tackle trafficking. One operation visited approximately 10 percent of known sex work establishments across the UK and identified 84 women and young people who were known to have been trafficked. Most were aged 18 to 25, but 12 were aged between 14 and 17 years. These women came from 22 countries, and the largest proportion was from Eastern Europe (Gloucestershire Police). Based on the fact that only 10 percent of sex work establishments were visited in the course of this investigation, the police estimated there was probably ten times the number of identified women who had been trafficked for CSE who had not yet been discovered.

Trafficked Children and Young People in the UK

The evidence regarding the origins of young people who are trafficked into Britain differs slightly from that of adult females. Research conducted by ECPAT UK in the North East, North West and West Midlands regions of England identified 80 cases of known or suspected trafficked children who had been taken into the care of social services. Of these the biggest proportion (45) were aged 16 to 17 years, but 22 were under 16. In 13 cases, age was not specified. Two-thirds (50) were female, approximately a quarter (19) was male and in eleven cases gender was not specified. Most of the young women had been trafficked for CSE or domestic servitude while the young men had been trafficked primarily for criminal activity although some had also been involved in sexual exploitation (ECPAT, 2007).

The majority of these young people originated from Africa and South East Asia (especially Nigeria and China). Disturbingly, once they had been taken into the care of social services, 60 percent (48) of these children went missing and have never been found. This pattern of trafficked young people going missing from care has been found in other areas of the country (ECPAT, 2001). Most go missing within the first 72 hours or one week of being taken into care and many go missing before they have been identified as victims of trafficking (ECPAT, 2007). ECPAT suggests the reasons for going missing are that they are still controlled by their traffickers who remove from the area as soon as possible or they run away in an attempt to escape their traffickers (ECPAT, 2007).

Evidence suggests that trafficking young people is a problem across the UK. When they go missing young people are moved around within the country (ECPAT, 2007; Kapoor, 2007). Indigenous youths are also known to be moved around in the UK for the purpose of CSE (Melrose, 2004), while internationally trafficked youths are also moved through the UK to other countries. In particular there has been a problem documented of young African girls being brought to the UK and then moved to Italy for CSE (ECPAT, 2001). A case of Chinese girls being moved to Canada has also been identified (ECPAT, 2007; q.v. Kapoor, 2007).

A scoping exercise conducted by the Child Exploitation Online Protection center (CEOP) identified 330 children who were suspected to have been trafficked into the UK. Of these, 85 cases were deemed to be "high probability" and 105 as "very high probability" (Kapoor, 2007). This study identified 44 source countries: in the Far East, South East Asia, Central Asia, South Asia, West Africa, Eastern Europe and the Baltic States (Kapoor, 2007; Carling, 2006). All the young people identified in this study were under 18 with the biggest proportion (85 percent) being 15 to 17 years of age. The purpose of trafficking and the type of intended exploitation was unclear in approximately two-thirds of the cases. However, in the "high and very high" probability categories 91 cases were female and of these two-thirds were believed to have been trafficked for CSE (Kapoor, 2007).

Responding to Trafficking in the UK and the U.S. Tier Ranking System

There is clearly a problem with trafficking of women and young people into, through and within the UK for CSE. From 2000–2007 the U.S. State Department's TIP report has rated the efforts of the UK to tackle this problem in Tier One. This means the UK is considered to be in full compliance with minimum standards for combating human trafficking (Women's Commission, 2005). So what has the UK done to warrant this evaluation of its efforts? Below I will outline domestic legal instruments and other initiatives that have been developed to combat human trafficking. I will then show how these developments are undermined by the British government's stance on immigration and asylum legislation and by its focus on border control and organized crime rather than the human rights abuses to which those who are trafficked are subjected.

Legislation

The first domestic legislation introduced to tackle human trafficking in recent times was part of the *Nationality, Asylum and Immigration Act*. This was a "stop-gap" measure (Dickson, 2004) which outlawed trafficking only in relation to prostitution. This was followed by the *Sexual Offenses Act (2003)*, which incorporated the provisions of the NAIA (2002) but expanded the notion of "sexual exploitation" to include forms of sexual exploitation other than prostitution. This legislation explicitly criminalized the CSE of those under 18 and recognized "trafficking" as something that can take place within national borders as well as across them. Under this legislation the maximum penalty for trafficking is 14 years imprisonment.

This legislation was followed by the *Asylum and Immigration (Treatment of Claimants) Act* (2004). This legislation fundamentally altered the asylum appeals process, placed further restrictions on eligibility criteria for receiving welfare benefits and increased penalties for using fraudulent documents for entering the country. It also extended definitions of trafficking to take into account exploitation for reasons other than CSE such as forced labor and domestic servitude. Further immigration legislation was enacted in 2006 in the *Immigration, Asylum and Nationality Act 2006*. This contained no specific measures to combat trafficking but further restricted the right of appeal for those refused entry to the UK and introduced measures to fine and/or imprison employers for employing illegal workers.

Other measures

In addition to legal instruments other initiatives have been developed to respond to human trafficking. In 2003 the Home Office produced a "Toolkit for People Trafficking" (www.crimereduction.gov.uk/toolkits/tp00.htm), and provided funding for The Poppy Project to support adult female victims of trafficking. However, this provided just 25 bed spaces and was the only facility of its kind in the country. Criteria for acceptance by the service were very strict: women had to be over 18 years old, had to have been working in prostitution in the UK for 30 days prior to referral, had to have been trafficked for CSE and had to be prepared to help the police to prosecute her traffickers by giving evidence. Women were given 30 days to decide whether to cooperate with the police and if they declined they would be returned to their country of origin (Taylor, 2005; Women's Commission, 2005).

Currently there is no dedicated support for young people (under 18) who are victims of trafficking. This is because campaigners have fought for them to be worked with under child protection procedures. Young people are thus referred to social services departments for support but grave doubts have been expressed about their ability to provide the dedicated support such young people need (Women's Commission, 2005; ECPAT, 2004; ICAR, 2007). Although the Department for Children, Schools and Families has just published welcome guidance on safeguarding children and young people thought to be trafficked (DCSF, 2008), this does not go far enough in saying what children's services should do to provide for the needs of trafficked young people. In addition to these developments, the government established as part of the police service, the UK Human Trafficking Centre

(UKHTC) and the CEOP service in 2006. The former gathers intelligence about all forms of national and international trafficking (but is primarily focused on trafficking for CSE) to support police operations in disrupting trafficking networks. CEOP is dedicated to eradicating all forms of child sexual abuse.

Two police operations (Pentameter I and II) to tackle trafficking were launched in 2006 and 2007. The results of the first are discussed above—those of the second are not yet available.

A Critical Review of UK Efforts

The UK government claims its approach to human trafficking is "victim centered" and it has developed the measures described above to combat trafficking. However, I argue that these efforts are enfeebled by the government's determination to impose ever stricter asylum regulations on those trying to escape discrimination, victimization, violence and/or poverty; many of whom are victims of trafficking (Women's Commission, 2005; ECPAT, 2007; Refugee Council, 2008). The tightening of asylum regulations and immigration controls suggests that the UK government is not primarily concerned with the human rights abuses endured by those who are subject to trafficking; instead it is concerned with controlling its borders and tackling organized crime (Refugee Council, 2006). Its approach is therefore arguably not victim centered.

Numerous studies have shown that the more difficult it is for people legally to leave areas where they experience human rights abuses, torture, persecution, discrimination and/or poverty, the more likely they are to turn to smuggling or trafficking networks to facilitate their escape (Andrijasevic, 2003; Monzini, 2005; Women's Commission, 2005; Carling, 2006; Moorehead, 2006; Mecham, 2006; Lee, 2007; Hudson, 2007; Grewcock, 2007; Refugee Council, 2008). By making asylum and immigration processes ever more restrictive, UK state practices have therefore inadvertently constructed the mercenary territory in which human traffickers and smugglers hunt and operate.

The UK government describes its response to trafficking as three-pronged. It aims to prosecute traffickers, protect victims and prevent trafficking by raising awareness of the issue at home and abroad. Its ability to protect victims, however, is undermined by punitive asylum and immigration legislation (Women's Commission, 2005; Refugee Council, 2008; ECPAT, 2007, 8). The UK government is reluctant to offer support to victims of trafficking believing this may encourage traffickers, swell the ranks of asylum seekers, encourage illegal immigration and/or provide an incentive for people who want to come to Britain to take advantage of its welfare system (Mynott, 2002). Support and protection of trafficking victims is emasculated because the UK has not adopted legal mechanisms to protect or support trafficking victims. Instead, they must qualify for asylum or humanitarian protection (Women's Commission, 2005). The Joint Committee for Human Rights recently criticized the government for its treatment of trafficking victims citing examples of arrest, detention and deportation (ICAR, 2007); subsequently the Prime Minister revealed his intention to sign the *Council of Europe Convention on Action against Trafficking in Human Beings* (2005).

Apart from the asylum process itself having become more stringently regulated, qualifying for asylum has also become more difficult as a result of the UK government's identification of a "white list" of countries. These are considered to be "safe" countries from which claims for asylum will not be considered. Although they considered "safe" by the UK government, many of these countries do not comply with the minimum standards defined by the United States government's *TVPA 2000* and they are not classified in Tier One. Instead, many of these countries are known as source areas for trafficking (Women's Commission, 2005).

As the Refugee Council (2008) and ECPAT (2007) have pointed out, asylum and immigration legislation does not only create problems for adults who are trafficked; there are also conflicts between immigration legislation and child protection. In this conflict the child's best interests are often subjugated to issues of immigration control.

In 1990 the UK ratified the *UN Convention on the Rights of the Child* (1989). Article 34 requires that states take steps to prevent the abduction, sale or trafficking of children for any purpose. While ratifying this Convention the British government entered a reservation allowing it to pass its own immigration legislation that would not need to take account of its obligations under the Convention (Women's Commission, 2005). This reservation removes the rights of children who have entered the country in an unorthodox way (ECPAT, 2007). In 2004 the Joint Committee on Human Rights pointed out that this reservation, "Appears to legitimize the unequal treatment of those vulnerable children by both central and local government (cited in Refugee Council, 2008, 5)."

Targets for the removal of unaccompanied asylum-seeking children have also been introduced and these are at odds with the idea that trafficking responses are "child centered" (ECPAT, 2007, 8). More worryingly still, the UK Immigration Service and the Home Office Immigration and Nationality Directorate are exempt from the statutory obligation, as set out in the *Children Act 2004*, to "have regard to safeguard and promote the welfare of children" (ECPAT, 2007, 13).

Conclusions

This chapter has argued that distinguishing human "smuggling" from "trafficking" is not as straightforward in practice as the law might suggest. This is because in reality human trafficking is an "untidy" process (ECPAT, 2007, 6) which is filled with complexity. While distinctions between smuggling and trafficking are important to allow governments to manage and control migration they are not necessarily helpful for victims of the trafficking process.

The evidence presented has demonstrated that there are problems in the UK in relation to trafficking both young people and adults. The UK is both a country of destination and transit although the evidence would suggest that it is less likely to be a country of transit for adults than it is for young people. The chapter has also shown that while adult trafficking victims are primarily Eastern European, young people tend to come from Africa and China.

The discussion has described the legislative mechanisms and other initiatives developed by the UK government since the turn of the twenty-first century. For the government, human trafficking represents a problem of border control and organized crime while for many others it represents an abuse of the human rights of people on a migratory journey. The chapter has argued that government efforts to combat human trafficking are undermined by restrictions imposed on asylum applications and a "crack down" on illegal immigrants. While the UK government may be compliant with U.S.-defined minimum standards for combating human trafficking it still has a long way to go in terms of offering support and protection to the victims of this trade. As the Women's Commission (2005, 22) has pointed out: "The efforts of the UK have not been combined into a unified, effective strategy that not only prevents, deters, and punishes trafficking, but, most importantly, embraces the rights and protection of trafficked persons."

References

Anderson, B., and O'Connell-Davidson, J. (2003). *Is Trafficking in Human Beings Demand Driven? A multi-country pilot study*, International Organization for Migration.

Andrijasevic, R. (2003). "The Difference Borders Make: (Il)Legality, Migration and 'Trafficking' into Italy among Eastern European Women in Prostitution," in Ahmed, S., Castaneda, C., Fortier, A. and Sheller, M. (eds.) *Uprootings/Regroundings: Questions of Home and Migration*, Oxford, Berg Publishers.

Brown, L. (2000). *Sex Slaves: The trafficking of women in Asia*, London, Virago.

Carling, J. (2006). *Migration, Human Smuggling and Trafficking from Nigeria to Europe*, IOM Migration Research Series No. 23, Geneva.

Dickson, S. (2004). *Sex in the City: Mapping Commercial Sex across London*, London, The Poppy Project/Eaves Housing for Women.

DCSF. (2008). *Safeguarding Children Who May Have Been Trafficked*, London, DCSF.

ECPAT. (2001). *What the Professionals Know: The trafficking of children into and through the UK for sexual purposes*, London, ECPAT UK.

ECPAT. (2004). *Cause for Concern: London Social Services and Child Trafficking* London, ECPAT UK.

ECPAT. (2007). *Missing Out: A study of child trafficking in the North West, North East and West Midlands*, London, ECPAT UK.

Experts Group on Trafficking in Human Beings. (2004). *Report of the Experts Group on Trafficking in Human Beings*, Brussels, European Commission Directorate—General Justice, Freedom and Security.

Futo, P., Jandl, M., and Karsakova, L. (2005). "Illegal Migration and Human Smuggling in Central and Eastern Europe," *Migracijske i etnicke teme* 21: 35–54.

Gallagher, A. (2001). "Human Rights and the New UN Protocols on Trafficking and Migrant Smuggling: A Preliminary Analysis, *Human Rights Quarterly*, 975–1004.

Grewcock, M. (2007). "Shooting the Passenger: Australia's war on illicit migrants" in M. Lee (ed.) *Human Trafficking*, Devon, Willan Publishing.

Hudson, B., (2007). "The Rights of Strangers: Policies, theories and philosophies" in M. Lee (ed.) ibid.

ICAR (2007). *Vulnerable Groups in the Asylum Determination Process: Thematic Briefing prepared for the Independent Asylum Commission*, Information Centre about Asylum and Refugees. <www.icar.org.uk> (30 Aug. 2008).

Iselin, B., and Adams, M. (2003). *Distinguishing between Human Trafficking and People Smuggling*, Bangkok, United Nations Office on Drugs and Crime.

Kangaspunta, K. (2003). *Mapping the Inhuman Trade*, Forum on Crime and Society. <www.unodc.org/pdf/crime/forum/forum3_note1.pdf> (30 Aug. 2009).

Kapoor, A. (2007). *A Scoping Project on Child Trafficking in the UK*, London, CEOP.

Kelly, L. (2007). "A conducive context: Trafficking of persons in Central Asia" in M. Lee (ed.) op. cit.

Kelly, L., and Regan, L. (2000). *Stopping Traffic: Exploring the Extent of, and Responses to, Trafficking in Women for Sexual Exploitation in the UK*, London, Home Office.

Laczko, F., and Gramegna, M. (2003). "Developing Better Indicators of Human Trafficking," *Brown Journal of World Affairs*, Vol. X, Issue 1.

Lee, M. (2007). "Introduction: Understanding Human Trafficking," in M. Lee (ed.) op. cit.

Lehti, M. (2003). *Trafficking in Women and Children in Europe*, Finland, (Heuni Papers No. 18) The European Institute for Crime Prevention affiliated with the United Nations.

Mecham, M. (2006). "Redeeming Stolen Lives: What role do NGOs play in confronting the trafficking of people into the UK?" *4th Annual Forced Migration Post-Graduate Student Conference*, University of East London, 18–19 March.

Melrose, M. (2004). "Of Tricks and Other Things: An Overview" in M. Melrose with D. Barrett, (eds.) *Anchors in Floating Lives: Interventions with Young People Sexually Abused through Prostitution*, Lyme Regis, Russell House Publishing.

Melrose, M., and Barrett, D. (2006). "The Flesh Trade in Europe: Trafficking in Women and Children for the purpose of Commercial Sexual Exploitation," *Police Practice and Research: An International Journal,* 7(2) Special Edition.

Monzini, P. (2005). *Sex Traffic: Prostitution, Crime and Exploitation,* London, ZED Books.

Moorehead, C. (2006). *Human Cargo: A Journey Among Refugees,* London, Vintage.

Morrison, J. (2004). *FMO Research Guide: Human Smuggling and Trafficking,* <www.forcedmigration.org/guides/fmo011> (30 Aug. 2008).

Mynott, E. (2002). "From a shambles to a new apartheid: local authorities, dispersal and the struggle to defend asylum seekers" in S. Cohen, B. Humphries, and E. Mynott (eds.) *From Immigration Controls to Welfare Controls,* London, Routledge.

Nieuwenhuys, C., and Pecoud, A. (2007). "Human Trafficking, Information Campaigns and Strategies of Migration Control," *American Behavioral Scientist* 50:1674.

O'Connell-Davidson, J. (2002). *The Borders of Contract: Trafficking and Migration,* ESRC Seminar Series, #2.

Refugee Council (2006). *Refugee Council Briefing: Trafficking in Persons.* <www.refugeecouncil.org.uk> (30 Aug. 2008).

Refugee Council (2008). *Human Trafficking—Refugee Council Response to the Home Affairs Select Committee Inquiry into Human Trafficking.* <www.refugeecouncil.org.uk> (30 Aug. 2008).

Salt, J. (2000). "Trafficking and Human Smuggling: A European Perspective," *International Migration,* 38 (1): 31–56.

Taylor, G. (2005). *Evaluation of the Victims of Trafficking Pilot Project—POPPY,* London, Home Office.

Women's Commission. (2005). *The Struggle between Migration Control and Victim Protection: The UK approach to Human Trafficking,* New York, Women's Commission for Refugee Women and Children.

7

Human Trafficking in Austria, Poland, and Croatia

Karin Bruckmüller and Stefan Schumann

AUSTRIA, POLAND (38.1 MILLIONS INHABITANTS) and Croatia (4.4 millions inhabitants), differ in their political history and economic situation. While Austria was part of the democratic and market economy driven western European hemisphere already during the cold war, Poland and Croatia were part of Eastern Europe. Poland, a Republic since 1918, established itself as a democratic state in 1989, and Croatia, a former part of the Republic of Yugoslavia, was recognized as an independent state in 1991–1992. Today, all three are members of the European Union (EU)—a context that has to be kept in mind because EU laws contain an individual's right of free movement within all of the EU territory. Furthermore, it establishes legal obligations on preventing and combating trafficking in human beings (THB), and the EU provides a framework for cooperation between EU institutions, governmental institutions, law enforcement agencies, as well as international and regional NGOs. Such closer cooperation is needed within the Schengen area where internal border controls are abolished between the EU Member States (excluding the UK and Ireland) as well as Norway, Switzerland and Iceland—a common external border control regime has therefore been established.

Regarding legislation and practical measures to combat THB all three states, including Croatia as an accession country, have to focus on the EU legal measures, comply with the respective convention and law of the Council of Europe (COE) and that of the UN's. Combating and preventing THB has been gaining political priority in Europe, with human trafficking viewed as a grave violation of human rights and human dignity. Therefore the above mentioned actors on the European level have taken a comprehensive and multidisciplinary approach to the fight against this phenomenon by adopting various instruments, such as legal rules (EU FD on Combating THB, 2002; EU FD on Combating Sexual Exploitation, 2004; COE Convention, 2005; EU Action Plan, 2005) and a series of programmes. The focus is on preventative measures, criminal prosecution, cooperation of police and judicial authorities, protection to, and assistance for victims, and general cooperative measures between national law enforcement agencies, EU institutions and NGOs. In EU *Framework Decision on Combating Trafficking in Human Beings*, human trafficking is defined as:

- an act of controlling a person by either using physical or mental violence, deceit or fraud or by abusing authority or a position of vulnerability or by exchange of payment to achieve the consent of a person having control over the victim
- for the purpose of labour or sexual exploitation of the trafficked person.

The consent of a victim of trafficking in human beings to the exploitation, intended or actual, is therefore irrelevant where any of the above mentioned means have been used.

Austria

Trafficking Routes, Exploitation

Resulting from the geographical location and its relative wealth, Austria is both a transit and a destination country for cross-border trafficking in human beings (Austrian Report on Combating THB, 2008). Romania, Bulgaria, Hungary, Slovakia, Georgia, and China are the source countries for trafficking (Pfanzelter, 2008), in addition to Nigeria and the Eastern European countries of Moldovia, Belarus, Ukraine (TIP, 2008). In cases where Austria is a transit country the victims are trafficked to Italy, France, and Spain (TIP, 2008).

According to estimates, the victims in Austria were trafficked predominantly for the purpose of sexual exploitation and forced labor in slave-like situations of domestic servants, including child trafficking (*Austrian Report on Combating Human Trafficking*, 2008). The victims of THB in Austria, usually come from less affluent countries; while other push factors include gender inequalities, domestic violence, lack of education or job possibilities in their country of origin, and poverty. The perception of increased opportunities in Austria, or in case of transit through Austria, in the country of destination is the main pull factor (*Europol Report*, 2006). Cases of child trafficking to or through Austria usually involve child victims from the above mentioned south eastern European countries (i.e., Bulgaria, Romania, Moldovia, Serbia, and Slovakia), but also from Africa and Latin America. Often those child victims were sold by their parents under false pretexts. Child trafficking is committed for the purpose of begging, thievery or pickpocketing, and/or for sexual exploitation as prostitutes, profit in adoptions, or for brokering marriage of minors (*Austrian Report on Child Trafficking*, 2008).

In 2007 there were only 18 cases, tried under Art. 104a Austrian Criminal Code, which prohibits trafficking in human beings—defined in accordance to the above mentioned *European Union Framework Decision*, but additionally includes trafficking for the purpose of removal of organs. It has to be kept in mind that cases concerning one of the other above mentioned offenses may also have an aspect of trafficking in human beings. This interaction is underlined by the following: In 2007, the Austrian victim support organization LEFÖ-IBF, specialized in supporting female victims of human trafficking, assisted 170 female migrants who came to Austria by means of trafficking (Pfanzelter, 2008).

Austria is classified as a Tier 1 country in the TIP reports (2001–2008), viz., the Austrian government fully complies with the Trafficking Victims Protection Act's (TVPA) minimum standards. Austria is actively involved in combating human trafficking by taking a comprehensive and interdisciplinary approach in preventing and sanctioning THB. The core elements of the Austrian strategy are the coordination of all activities concerned at the regional, national and international level by awareness raising, the protection of victims by establishing victims' rights as well as specialized victim support organizations, and the prosecution of the offenders of THB and those who instigate, aid, or abet or attempt to commit such an act.

Austria has signed and ratified all relevant international treaties on combating human trafficking, such as the *UN Convention against Transnational Organized Crime* and its *Protocol to Prevent, Suppress, and Punish Trafficking in Persons, Especially Women and Children* (adopted in 2000), and *Council of Europe Convention on Action against Trafficking in Human Beings* (2005). Austria was the first COE Member State, which ratified the criminalization of human trafficking in accordance to the above mentioned conventions and the legally binding EU Framework Decisions (Reiter, 2008). In order to take additional necessary and practical measures to prevent THB and to reduce harm to the victims, a working group—the Task Force on Human Trafficking—was established and the national Action Plan against Human Trafficking was drafted.

To prevent trafficking in human beings and to identify victims of human trafficking it is important to raise the awareness of the public as well as the law enforcement agencies. A number of events were organized and attracted a lot of media attention. For instance Austria supported the "UN.GIFT—Vienna Forum to Fight Human Trafficking." Special training courses, initiated by the Ministry of Interior are intended to raise awareness of the law enforcement agencies involved in combating trafficking in human beings. These courses aim to identify the victims and to communicate psychological needs of those victims to police and border control officers. The police come in contact with victims of human trafficking, when suspected as offenders of migration rules, or as perpetrators of criminal offenses as thefts or pickpocketing. Once a victim is perceived and treated as an offender, such perception might obscure their status as victims of trafficking in human beings. Moreover, the identification of child victims of trafficking in human beings is sometimes endangered by an impossibility to differentiate clearly between unaccompanied refugee minors, unaccompanied alien minors, minors who entered the country with the help of human smugglers, and victims of trafficking in human beings (Austrian Report on Child Trafficking, 2008). The training, therefore, aims to sensitize the police officers that the person could be a trafficked victim and therefore the police officer should involve an officer trained to handle vulnerable crime victims. The training of border control officers aimed also to improve the ability to identify human trafficking victims. In order to cooperate with the government or law enforcement agencies in the countries of origin there is an ongoing international exchange of information and experiences.

Austria tries to offer comprehensive professional support to victims of human trafficking. Especially LEFÖ-IBF as the nationwide victim support organization specialized in supporting female victims of human trafficking offers or coordinates comprehensive (social, psychological and medical) treatments, and provide psychosocial and legal assistance to victims during criminal proceedings (*Austrian Report on Combating Human Trafficking*, 2008). They are mostly the first contact point for child victims (or even male victims) and liaison with other victim support organizations. Victim support organizations also try to cooperate with the source countries to ensure a safe return of the victims and their rehabilitation in the home country. Additionally, public prosecutors are trained to deal with the mostly vulnerable victims of THB in accordance with the Austrian Action Plan on Human Trafficking. A witness protection program has been established by the Federal Ministry of the Interior, if the victim has a potential of being endangered because of his/her willingness to cooperate with the police (Pfanzelter, 2008).

Austria may be called a "model country" (Austrian Report on Combating Human Trafficking, 2008) as regards victims' protection because Austria grants to the victims a temporary residence permit for a period of 30 days to recover and reflect, which is not made conditional on the victims' ability or willingness to cooperate with the authorities. Austria receives no direct funding from the United States. However, a U.S. Fulbright student was supported to conduct research on immigration and trafficking (United States Government Funding, 2006).

Poland

Poland, an EU Member State, is a transit and destination country for victims of trafficking largely due to its geographical location between the more affluent western EU countries and the poorer states of the former Soviet Union; and it is also a country of origin. Trafficking victims originate in Armenia, Azerbaijan, Belarus, Bulgaria (a large number are of the Turkish minority in Southern Bulgaria), Moldovia, Romania (many from the Roma/Sinti population), Russia, and Ukraine, and some from Kenya, Senegal, Sri Lanka and Costa Rica (Data of National Public Prosecutor's Office). Sexual exploitation as prostitutes is the main reason for the trafficking (The Protection Project, Report Poland). The victims were brought to or through Poland to western countries (mostly Austria, Belgium, Denmark, Germany, Greece, Italy, the Netherlands, Spain, Sweden), and Japan (U.S. Department). In cases where Poland is a country of origin, women are trafficked to Western Europe, Japan and North America for the purpose of commercial sexual exploitation (CSE), while some Polish men and women are trafficked to Italy, Austria, Germany, Belgium, France, Spain, Sweden, the Netherlands, and Israel for purposes of forced labor (TIP, 2008).

TABLE 7.1
Outcome of the Preparatory Proceedings in Cases Dealing with Trafficking in Human Beings in 1995–2008

YEAR	Number of completed cases	Number of cases resulting in bringing an indictment	Number of cases resulting in a discontinuance due to		Number of persons	
			Not detecting an offence	Not pronouncing an offence	charged	aggrieved
2005	31	19	2	10	42	99
2006	26	17	-	9	36	126
2007	48	28	1	19	62	1021
2008	53	28	4	21	78	315

In Poland human trafficking is punishable under the criminal code for "forced prostitution," "pimping," and "trafficking."

The number of victims protected by the Police is between 0–11 persons per year (see table above by the National Public Prosecutor's Office). The "La Strada" Foundation, an NGO actively involved in supporting victims of human trafficking, assisted in the last years the following numbers of victims, trafficked to or through Poland or originated in Poland (National Public Prosecutor's Office):

- 2005—224 persons (including 147 Polish women)
- 2006—230 persons (including 198 Polish women)
- 2007—276 persons (including 200 Polish women).

Since 2002, Poland has been a Tier 1 country, except for 2001 when it slipped to Tier 2. But Poland made significant efforts to bring itself into compliance with the TVPA's minimum standards: it ratified all the relevant international treaties and in the last few years made substantial progress to implement legal instruments, especially provisions on the protections of victims of THB (Council of Europe Report, 2007). In 2003, the government adopted the "National Programme for Combating and Preventing Trafficking in Human Beings" and one year later, the "Inter-Ministerial working group on Combating and Preventing Trafficking in Human Beings" was established (members are representatives of the government, experts from the police and experts from the relevant NGOs).

Victim support organizations offer a broad range of help-programs, with social support, such as accommodation, medical and legal services as well as emotional support (La Strada, see homepage above). They closely cooperate with crises intervention centres to ensure a fast and individual help (Buchowska, 2007). They also try to ensure a safe return to the victim's home country. Espe-

FIGURE 7.1
Tier Rankings for Poland (2001–2008)

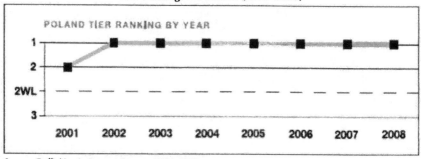

Source: Trafficking in Persons Reports, 2001–2008

cially the La Strada Foundation is engaged in the prevention of THB. It aims to reduce Polish victims by establishing education campaigns to empower women and providing them knowledge of their rights by especially targeting groups such as young and/or unemployed women and sex workers, and staff members also visit schools (La Strada, see homepage above). Law enforcement staff, such as the police, the border control forces and prosecutors are given special guidelines on how to identify a trafficked person (Buchowska, 2007). Victims of THB can apply for a temporary residence permit with a reflection period (60 days) provided for trafficked persons. A program of victim-witness support exists for persons who cooperate with the law enforcement agencies (Buchowska, 2007).

Croatia

Croatia is a country of transit and to a lesser extent, a destination country for female victims of trafficking (Commission Report, 2008). Predominantly women from Bulgaria, Hungary, Romania, Slovakia, and the Ukraine are trafficked to or through Croatia to France, Italy, Spain, and Switzerland for the purpose of CSE. Especially during the high tourist seasons in the Dalmatian coast THB rises (The Protection Project, Report Croatia). There is little information available on Croatian women victims of CSE in Western Europe (Limanowska, 2005). Croatia was involved in the Balkan War, which fueled human trafficking (The Protection Project, Report Croatia); Croatia is now relatively affluent in comparison with other countries of the region (Limanowska, 2005).

The Croatian Criminal Code stipulates the following offences as punishable: slavery, trafficking, international prostitution, and pandering. The number of female victims of THB rose from 7 in 2002 to 18 in 2003 (Limanowska, 2005) and 17 in 2004 (The Protection Project, Report Croatia). There is no data for 2005 and 2006 available. While the EU reports about

FIGURE 7.2
Tier Rankings for Croatia (2001–2008)

Source: Trafficking in Persons Reports, 2001–2008

13 victims in 2007 (Council of Europe Report, 2007), the United States named a number of 15 victims (TIP, 2008).

While Croatia was a Tier 2 ranked country for five years (2003–2007), and in 2004 was even on the Watch List, it has made improvements and achieved the Tier 1 ranking by 2008. Thus it complies fully to the TVPA's minimum standards: "A good progress has been made in the fight against trafficking in human beings (Commission Report, 2008)." A national Action Plan to combat human trafficking and an Action Plan for implementation of the migration policy was adopted by the government; and guidelines on how to handle cases of human trafficking were elaborated by the Ministry of Interior and the Ministry of Social Services (Commission Report, 2008). The core elements of these plans and guidelines are to prevent THB by education, identification of victims, prosecuting and sanctioning of offenders, assistance to victims, and coordination of activities.

A range of workshops and training programs on the human trafficking were organized for agencies involved in combating THB (Commission Report, 2008)—such as the Center for Social Policy for prevention of child victims of trafficking (Limanowska, 2005)—along with capacity-building workshops organized for IGOs, NGOs, and governmental agencies (The Protection Project, Report Croatia). A range of awareness initiatives were established focusing on prevention: women's economic empowerment programs were developed (Commission Report, 2008), and an educational program on preventing trafficking was set up in Croatian high schools (The Protection Project, Report Croatia). ROSA, a local NGO, supports victims of THB by providing legal, medical and psychological services, along with witness protection (TIP, 2008). According to the Law of Foreigners a potential adult victim of THB is provided with a 30 day reflection period while the temporary residence permit is up to 90 days for child victims.

Conclusion

Although there are already a lot of workshops and training programs especially for police officers and border control staff, one of the challenges still remaining is the identification of victims of THB. Another challenge is the collection and availability of (comparable) data, not only at the regional, but also at the international level. There is a need of a clear common definition of human trafficking and comparable indicators for such data collection. To solve this problem Austria takes part in a wide ranging project on harmonizing data collection on human trafficking within the EU. Austria, Croatia and Poland follow a comprehensive and interdisciplinary approach preventing and combating human trafficking. This strategy includes preventative measures, sanctioning of offenders, support of victims, and cooperation of authorities and civil society involved. This approach is to be recognized on a European level as well as on a bilateral and a intrastate level. Regional EU law and the accompanying Action plan, in accordance with international treaties, establish a minimum standard on legal and practical measures: the exchange of information between law enforcement agencies including the EU institutions Europol and Eurojust contributes to detect transit routes and organized crime groups involved. Additionally, transnational cooperation, especially effective cooperation between source, transit and destination countries, contributes to the prevention of human trafficking by fighting push factors and by awareness raising and improves the combat of human trafficking.

References

Buchowska, S. (2007). *Social Aspects of Human Trafficking.* <http://www.peer-review-social-inclusion> (15 Feb. 2009).

Limanowska, B. (2005). *Trafficking in Human Beings in South Eastern Europe: Situation and Responses to Trafficking in Human Beings in Albania, Bosnia and Herzegovina, Bulgaria, Croatia, the Former Yugoslav Republic of Macedonia, Moldova, Serbia and Montenegro, including the UN Administered Province of Kosovo and Romania.* <http://www.osce.org/publications/odihr/2005/04/13771_211_en.pdf> (15 Feb. 2009).

Pfanzelter, G. (2008). *Statement at the General Assembly Thematic Debate on Human Trafficking.* <http://www.un.org/ga/president/62/ThematicDebates/humantrafficking/austria.pdf> (15 Feb. 2009).

Reiter, S. (2008). *Europäische Union und österreichisches Strafrecht : unter besonderer Berücksichtigung der Delikte gegen Menschenhandel und Schlepperei.*

Reports

Commission of the European Communities (2008), *Croatia 2008 Progress Report,* SEC (2008) 2694, <http://www.ipex.eu/ipex/webdav/site/myjahiasite/groups/Central-Support/public/2008/SEC_2008_2694/COM_SEC(2008)2694_EN.pdf> (15 Feb. 2009)Council of Europe, 2007. *Memorandum to the Polish Government Assessment of the progress made in implementing the 2002 recommendations of the Council of Europe Commissioner for Human Rights,* 13, <https://wcd.coe.int/ViewDoc.jsp?id=1 155005&BackColorInternet=FEC65B&BackColorIntranet=FEC65B&BackColorLogged=FFC679#P326_50804> (15 Feb. 2009).

Europol Report on Trafficking of women and children for sexual exploitation in the EU: The *involvement of western Balkans organised crime 2006.* <http://www.europol.europa.eu/publications/Serious_Crime_Overviews/Western_Balkans_THB_Threat_Assessment.PDF> (15 Feb. 2009).

Final Daphne Report (2004). <http://ec.europa.eu/justice_home/daphnetoolkit/files/ projects/2004_1_075/2004_1_075_final_report_en.doc> (15 Feb. 2009).

First Austrian Report on Combating Human Trafficking (2008). <https://cms.bmeia. at/fileadmin/user_upload/bmeia/First_Austrian_Report_in_THB_080730.pdf> (15 Feb. 2009).

Johns Hopkins University, *The Protection Project, Report Croatia,* www.protectionproject.org/programs/tpp/europe_central_asia.htm.

———. *The Protection Project, Report Poland:* www.protectionproject.org/programs/ tpp/europe_central_asia.htm.

Report by the Working Group on Child Trafficking under the Task Force on Human Trafficking—Prevention of trafficking in children and protection of the victims of child trafficking (2008): https://cms.bmeia.at/en/foreign-ministry/foreign-policy/ human-rights/main-human-rights-issues/combatting-human-trafficking.html, (Austrian Report on Child Trafficking, 2008).

Treaties

Council of Europe (2005), Convention on Action against Trafficking in Human Beings, ETS No. 197 (COE Convention, 2005).

European Union (2004), Directive 2004/80/EC of 29 April 2004 relating to compensation to crime victims, (EU Directive, 2004).

European Union (2002), Framework Decision 2002/629/JHA on Combating Trafficking in Human Beings (EU FD on Combating THB, 2002).

European Union (2004), Framework Decision 2004/68/JHA on Combating the Sexual Exploitation of Children and Child Pornography (EU FD on Combating Sexual Exploitation, 2004).

European Union (2005), Plan on best practices, standards and procedures for combating and preventing trafficking in human beings, 2005/C 311/01 (EU Action Plan, 2005).

United Nations Convention (2002) against Transnational Organized Crime and its Protocol to Prevent, Suppress, and Punish Trafficking in Persons, Especially Women and Children (UN Convention, 2002).

IV

NEAR EAST

Kimberly A. McCabe and Sabita Manian

A TTENTION TO THE COUNTRIES IN THE Near East in terms of their economic and political influences in the United States has done little to alleviate the problem of sex trafficking. In fact, as American officials turn their focus to the desperately needed resources found in those countries, it appears as though we are able to overlook certain criminal activities if we can maintain our close ties with those countries. At the same time, sex trafficking continues with few new anti-trafficking efforts initiated. The two chapters in this section—one on Algeria and Morocco and the other on the Gulf States—provide further details on sex trafficking in this region. During 2005, countries in the Near East region initiated three new or amended legislative acts to reduce human trafficking; in 2006, these countries initiated two legislative acts and, in 2005, only one. Prosecutions of cases of sex trafficking have dropped from approximately 1,000 in 2003 to less than 300 in 2006 and, in 2008, none of the countries within the Near East region were classified as a Tier 1 country. Therefore, to report that sex trafficking is a problem in the Near East is certainly an understatement.

The geographic region of the Near East has one of the largest workforces in the world. Algeria's efforts to reduce human trafficking remain at a minimum. In fact, Algeria does not prohibit all forms of trafficking and often places its only efforts on reducing child sex trafficking. In addition, Algeria provides little protection for those identified victims of sex trafficking and in many cases victims are either deported or punished. In terms of participation in the sex market, the United States specifically identified Saudi Arabia and Kuwait as two countries in which victims of sex trafficking have been identified on numerous occasions but with no response from their governments (McCabe, 2008). The government of Kuwait has not developed any comprehensive anti-trafficking national plan or specific anti-trafficking legislation. In addition, efforts to assist victims of sex trafficking are minimum with victims often unable to pursue legal justice and, in some cases, victims are returned to their traffickers (U.S. Department of State, 2004). The government of Saudi Arabia has failed to enact any sort of comprehensive anti-trafficking law and although evidence exists to suggest a significant number of cases of sex trafficking, law enforcement does not put forth efforts to reduce sexual exploitation or to provide protection to victims of sex trafficking (U.S. Department of State, 2007). Therefore, victimization through sex trafficking continues in Saudi Arabia with victims often punished by not only their traffickers, but also by the government that may deport them. Finally, it is suggested that victims of sex trafficking in the Near East only receive help if they can assist the prosecution in the conviction of their traffickers (Limanowska, 2005) and in some cases the victims of sex trafficking are themselves punished by execution.

In this section, it is also suggested that organized crime plays a significant role in sex trafficking in the Near East (McCabe, 2008). In Israel, for example, it is suggested that as many as 20 percent of the foreign workers are victims of sex trafficking. In Morocco, authorities are discovering more and more cases of children being sold by their parents to organized human traffickers. In a culture with little value placed on women and children and little in terms of legislative or police efforts to reduce human trafficking, the criminal activity of sex trafficking continues and, as noted, flourishes. The two chapters in this section discuss the problems of human trafficking in the selected Near East countries and the countries' inattention to the criminal activity of sex trafficking.

References

Limanowska, B. (2005). "The Victim Perspective—Neglected Dimensions" in Sector Project Against Trafficking *Challenging Trafficking in Persons: Theoretical Debate and Practical Approaches*. Nomas, Baden-Baden.

McCabe, K. (2008). *The Trafficking of Persons: National and International Responses*. NY: Peter Lang.

U.S. Department of State (2004, June). *Trafficking in Persons: Report*. Washington, DC: Office to Monitor and Combat Trafficking in Persons.

U.S. Department of State (2007, June). *Trafficking in Persons*. Report. Washington, DC: Office to Monitor and Combat Trafficking in Persons.

8

The Wretched of the Earth:
Trafficking, the Maghreb, and Europe

Sunita Manian

A L MAGHREB, WHICH MEANS "THE WEST" IN Arabic, consists of the three countries in North West Africa: Morocco, Algeria and Tunisia. Conquered by the
Arab Ummayids in the seventh century, who converted the native Berber to
Islam, the ethnic composition of the Maghreb today is Arab and Berber. Given
the dominance of Arabs in recent Maghrebi history, Arabic is the predominant
language of the Maghreb, while Berber, French and in the case of Morocco,
Spanish is also spoken by various subgroups. The political institutions after
decolonization range from a monarchy in Morocco to varying degrees of plural-
ism with a concentration of power in the Presidency in Algeria and Tunisia.

In 711 C.E., the Berber general Tariq Ibn Zyad set sail across the Mediterranean, ushering in a 700 year epoch in Andalusian Spain that among other
things produced the splendor of the al-Hambra, resurrected the works of the
ancient Greeks, and fashioned the Spanish guitar. While modern Spain takes
legitimate pride in the ancient glories of al Andalus, thirteen centuries later,
contemporary Mediterranean crossings from the coast of Africa is often considered a far more ignoble affair. Within this context this chapter will highlight the ways in which social realities such as linguistic hegemonies, gender
and religion; economic, colonial and neocolonial policies; and political exi-
gencies such as maintaining colonial ties to Europe determine the nature and
causes of trafficking. The migrants making this perilous journey by sea or by
other means face dangers ranging from the capsizing of frail boats in the high
seas to arrest by border enforcement agents of Southern Europe and North
Africa (Human Rights Watch, 2008). This chapter will focus attention on the

thousands who attempt to migrate to Europe either from, or transiting through, the countries of the Maghreb, especially those who are trafficked for sexual purposes and exploited physically, sexually and psychologically.

In the destination countries of Europe, on the one hand the social reality of an aging population and low fertility rates create the demand for labor, making migration an attractive proposition for those from the nonindustrialized world. On the other hand, notwithstanding the economics of borders allowing the free flow of goods and services, the political discourse in the industrialized world promotes the notion of the sanctity of borders and a perceived threat from foreign hordes. These contradictory threads result in highly lucrative prospects for clandestine networks established to enable migrants to overcome border security even as they are lured by the promise of economic opportunities in the industrialized world. This chapter will underscore the ways in which the economic, social and political interests of the destination countries of Europe, rather than the rights of victims, have shaped the discourse and policy on trafficking.

Nature of Trafficking

According to the U.S. State Department's 2008 Trafficking in Persons (TIP) report, trafficking in Algeria involves the transit of trafficked persons from sub-Saharan Africa into Portugal, France, Spain, Italy and Malta. Within Algeria many of the estimated 9,000 trafficked persons are forced to work as commercial sex workers in the case of women, or manual laborers in the case of men, in order to pay the traffickers (TIP, 2008, 55). Unlike Algeria where few Algerians are themselves victims of trafficking, *Morocco* is a source as well as transit and destination country for trafficked persons. Moroccan children are trafficked internally for the purposes of sexual exploitation in the sex tourism industry (Kandela, 2000) and domestic labor market; Moroccan women from rural areas seeking domestic work in urban centers often end up in situations of domestic servitude and face threats of physical and sexual violence; and Moroccan women and girls are trafficked for sexual exploitation both internally within Morocco and externally to Saudi Arabia, Qatar, Syria, UAE and European countries (TIP, 2008, 186). As with Algeria, Morocco also serves as a transit country for migrants from South Asia and North and sub-Saharan Africa who enter the country voluntarily, albeit illegally, en route to destinations in Europe, but who end up in the commercial sex trade and/or domestic servitude (TIP, 2007, 222). The 2007 TIP report notes the existence of internal trafficking of children and the arrest and conviction of 5 Dutch citizens in the Netherlands for sex tourism with minors in Tunisia (187).

In the receiving countries of Europe the demand for trafficked persons is driven by the sex industry where women and children trafficked from North Africa and sub-Saharan Africa service Europeans looking for an "exotic" experience. According to an expert at the United States Embassy in Madrid, there is an increasing demand for Arabic speaking sex workers to service the large number of clientèle from the Arab Middle East visiting Spain (Personal conversation, Elizabeth Fritschle, May 2008). Of the estimated 18,000 sex workers in France, a majority are believed to be victims of trafficking (TIP, 2008, 119), and between 3000–8000 trafficked children are believed to be engaged in commercial sex work, forced labor and begging. Within France, Maghrebi women trafficked into the sex industry mostly work in the port city of Marseille (Campani, 2004). Italy, with anywhere between 18,000–28,000 foreign sex workers, has considerably larger numbers of trafficked individuals than France or Spain, with an estimated 1,590 to 3,180 African victims living in that country. Trafficked sex workers solicit clients either through street prostitution (as in Italy) or clubs, bars and apartments (as in Spain). In France, trafficking victims practice both on and off street prostitution (Campani, 2004).

Causes of Trafficking

The primary reason for the existence of trafficking is economic, where the financial necessities of those trying to escape poverty in the "sending countries" is matched by a demand for labor caused by an aging population and decreasing fertility rates in the "receiving countries." High debt burden and financial instability in the 1980s led to IMF imposed Structural Adjustment Programs (SAPs) in Morocco, Algeria and Tunisia, which included measures to liberalize and privatize the economy. The consequent removal of agricultural subsidies, price supports, import controls, and the sale of public sector enterprises led to increased unemployment in many sectors of the economy (Davis, 2006; White, 2007). Simultaneously, trade agreements with EU countries and the United States of America have led to greater competition for Maghrebi producers from imports, while EU and U.S. subsidies, particularly those amounting to nearly one billion U.S. dollars a day to the agricultural sector deny Maghrebi farmers vital access to those markets.

In the immediate aftermath of decolonization, colonial ties to France had determined the economic and labor agreements by countries of the Maghreb. France's economic interests in Algeria, in particular oil concessions, put Algeria in a better bargaining position compared to its Maghrebi neighbors when it came to negotiating the rights of its nationals working in France. While the need for labor opened the doors of Europe to migrants from the Maghreb, the presence of North Africans, simultaneously gave rise to nationalistic and racist politics in the form of National Front in France and Lega Nord and Alleanza Nazionale in Italy (Collinson, 1996). With the incursion of these parties into mainstream politics by the late eighties and nineties, the discourse on immigration was no longer framed as an issue of labor-relations, but instead took the form of a fear of terrorism and perceived threat to national culture in the form of Islam. This in turn led to a tightening of immigration legislation and border security at the very time that SAPs were giving rise to an increasingly impoverished and desperate population in the Maghreb.

The social reasons that have led to internal and cross-border trafficking include discriminatory policies in Morocco against its Berber population, such as the imposition of Arabic and the suppression of Berber dialects (Aslan, 2007). This, in addition to the lack of infrastructure investment in the Berber areas, effectively denies economic opportunities to that population. Social practices such as male ownership of property, divorce by repudiation, lack of alimony since marriage ceremonies are traditional rather than legal or because the women lack identity papers, make women particularly vulnerable economically (Sater, 2007; Venema, 2004). When economic crises hit, such as the fallout from SAPs, women and their children fall prey to traffickers in their desperation to find alternative sources of income. Thus, trafficking from the Maghreb to Europe should be seen within the context of colonial relations and neocolonial policies such as SAPs and trade policy that advantages industrialized economies over those of the Maghreb; the political discourse in the industrialized nations that views all potential migrants as threats to security, culture and society; and social realities in the Maghreb that include ethnic discrimination and gender disempowerment.

Anti-Trafficking Measures

Among the sending or transit countries of the Maghreb, since 2007, the State Department has listed Algeria under Tier 3, downgraded from Tier 2 and Tier 2 Watch Lists in 2005 and 2006, respectively. The Algerian government is criticized for doing little to investigate incidents of or enforce laws against sex trafficking even though Algeria's anti-pimping laws under Articles 342–344 could be used for those purposes. Algeria also lacks initiatives for protecting the victims of trafficking, including lack of training of government officials in recognizing and handling of victims of trafficking and providing them with the appropriate physical and psychological care. Undocumented migrants, some caught in the commercial sale of sex, are deported or prosecuted even when they are merely the victims forced to ply their trade by traffickers. Furthermore, Algeria makes no attempt to use the testimony of the victims to prosecute traffickers (TIP, 2008, 56).

While Morocco was listed as a Tier 2 country when the State Department first started reporting on trafficking, from 2005–2007 the Moroccan government's efforts to stem and prosecute trafficking led to the country being ranked as Tier 1. Morocco's successes regarding trafficking, according to the TIP reports, have stemmed from several governmental initiatives aimed at rooting out the causes of trafficking. In 2003, Morocco adopted a new family code which abolished child marriages, established 18 as the age of consent for marriage, and granted women the ability to initiate divorce; additionally, in 2002, a 10 percent quota for women in the parliament was introduced as a means for empowering women. As a source country for trafficking, such laws are key to alleviating the conditions underlying gender disparities, which in turn fuel such social ills such as trafficking. Morocco also signed agreements with the IOM enabling them to open offices in Morocco, and established a bilateral commission with Spain to tackle trafficking. The Office of International Cooperation and the National Observatory of Migration were established in 2003 and 2004, respectively, to enforce anti-trafficking legislation (TIP, 2004, 199; TIP, 2005, 160). In July 2007, the IOM trained personnel from 25 ministries in Morocco on measures to counter human trafficking, and personnel from several international NGOs on effective strategies for information campaigns raising awareness of the dangers of trafficking.

Due to paucity of data little information is included by the State Department on Tunisia in most of the seven years under study, except in 2006 when Tunisia was placed under Tier 2. According to the most recent information available from the State Department on the country, Tunisia does not have a comprehensive law that could be applied to prosecute cases of human trafficking in all its forms. While Article 233 of the Tunisian penal code can be applied to prosecute cases of forced prostitution, it is rarely used. Most egregiously, the Tunisian government has not put in place any mechanism designed to distinguish between illegal migration and victims of trafficking, which often results in the latter being prosecuted for engaging in sexual labor. However, in cases where trafficking victims have been identified, the government has made provisions for the availability of social services, such as assigning "government workers, including social workers, to assist in three shelters for abused women and children operated by the Tunisian National Women's Union" (TIP, 2007, 222). Also, each district in Tunisia is assigned a "child protection delegate" to ensure access to medical and psychological care for child victims of sexual abuse. Tunisia is also commended by the TIP report for its collaborative efforts with receiving countries of Europe, such as Italy, including joint efforts at apprehending human traffickers. Furthermore, Tunisia also works with European governments to provide "social attachés" for Tunisian workers residing in those countries in order to disseminate pertinent information to its nationals, aimed at preventing their abuse and exploitation. (TIP, 2007, 222)

Among the receiving countries, Italy and Spain have consistently been ranked as Tier 1 countries since 2001. France was ranked as Tier 2 in 2001 due to a lack of measures aimed at protecting the victims of trafficking, who were prosecuted as illegal immigrants and either incarcerated or deported. However, in the following year, the State Department cited several initiatives by the French government, such as the appointment of an *Aide Sociale à l'Enfance*, who was charged with assisting underage victims of trafficking procure medical, psychological and legal aid, which earned France a place in Tier 1, a rank that it continues to hold (TIP, 2003, 49). In 2003 Italy, Spain and France each passed comprehensive laws that criminalized human trafficking. In the case of Italy and Spain this has included imposing jail terms of 8–20 years, and 5–12 years for traffickers, respectively. France's Domestic Security Law of 2003 entails the arrest and prosecution of victims of trafficking, including jail terms and deportations, under the arguably dubious notion that this would discourage trafficking. All three countries make provisions for granting temporary (France and Italy) or permanent (Spain) residence permits to trafficking victims who help to prosecute traffickers (TIP, 2007). Article 18 of Italy's Immigration Law stands out as one of the few statutes that allows the victim of trafficking to obtain a temporary work permit even if (s)he does not testify against traffickers (Campani, 2004; Berman, 2004, 51–53). Preventive measures against trafficking in Europe have included media campaigns targeting the demand side of trafficking, namely clients of sex workers. Government run Air France, in concert with NGOs focusing on prevention child sex abuse, includes information discouraging sex tourism emphasizing that engaging in sex with minors even in a foreign country is illegal under French Law. The Italian and Spanish government use advertisements, bumper stickers and posters to draw the link between trafficking and prostitution. For instance, a campaign in Madrid uses the slogan: "Because you pay, prostitution exists" (TIP, 2007, 187). While these campaigns target trafficking for sexual purposes, they do not, however, address other aspects of demand for labor.

Conclusion

Recent multilateral treaties addressing trafficking, such as the *UN Trafficking Protocol*, the *EU Framework Decision on Combating Trafficking in Human Beings*, and the *U.S. Trafficking Victims Protection Act*, have emerged in response to industrialized nations' fear of organized crime and the transgression of national borders by illegal migration (Pearson, 2005). Within this construct the emphasis remains overwhelmingly in favor of prosecuting the perpetrators of trafficking and/or illegal migration, subordinating the interests of victims of trafficking to security goals of the receiving countries (Pearson, 2005; Zimic, 2004; Pajnic, 2004). Victims of trafficking are often treated as such only if they help in prosecuting the traffickers (Limanowska, 2005). Furthermore, as underscored in the previous section, measures to address the demand for trafficking exclusively focus on the clients of sex workers, but direct little attention to employers who exploit other forms of labor. Indeed, the UN *International Convention on the Protection of the Rights of All Migrant Workers and Members of Their Families* has not been ratified by a single country in the industrialized world. Lastly, the current anti-trafficking measures are criticized for paternalistically restricting the freedom of movement of women across national borders.

The Human Rights approach to trafficking argues that the protection of the human rights of the victims should take center-stage in any anti-trafficking framework. Thus, this approach would eschew the current policy of most European countries, which accord temporary visas to victims in exchange for evidence leading to the prosecution of traffickers, in favor of providing such visas, along with access to psychological counseling and social services, to all victims whether or not they testify against traffickers. Furthermore, this approach argues for treating sex work as any other form of labor, where sex workers are viewed as agents capable of making decisions regarding their labor, so that trafficking only includes those instances where prostitution takes place under exploitative conditions (Berman, 2004).

According to Berman "trafficking narratives are also immigration stories" (2004, 48), where trafficking victims often have a "migration project," aimed at meeting a larger financial goal, and may even seek out smugglers to help bypass border security. It is when the relationship between the smuggler and migrant turn abusive and/or exploitative that the migrant is considered to be trafficked according to the anti-trafficking protocols. Critics argue that a person entering a country as a smuggled illegal migrant could become trafficked or vice versa, making the distinction between the two types of migrant unclear. The Migrant Rights Approach would argue that the language of the international anti-trafficking protocols makes a false dichotomy between the two kinds of labor (trafficked and smuggled), and would make a case for legislation that protects the rights of all migrant workers whether they live in a country legally or illegally.

Lastly, anti-trafficking policy should remain cognizant of the economic, social and political roots of trafficking. The current economic structures, including bilateral trade policy and structural adjustment programs are stacked against the interests of non-industrialized nations, creating an increasing impoverished citizenry willing to take incredible risks to escape poverty. The feminization of poverty due to lack of economic opportunities for women makes them, and their children, doubly vulnerable in this crisis, making them easy prey for traffickers. While the demand for labor in Europe draws migrants, increasing restrictions based on nationalistic fears makes the legal movement of labor tenuous. Thus, a holistic approach to the problem would have to include measures to alleviate the economic and social causes of trafficking and provide avenues for the legal migration of labor from North Africa to Europe.

References

Aslan, S. 2007. "Negotiating National Identity: Kurdish and Berber Rights Activism in Turkey and Morocco." Conference Papers, American Political Science Association Annual Meeting, 2007.

Berman, J. 2004. "Media constructions and migration projects," in S.Z. Zimic (ed.) *Women and Trafficking.* Peace Institute, Ljubljana.

Campani, G. 2004. "Trafficking for sexual exploitation in Southern Europe: realities and policies" in S.Z. Zimic (ed) *Women and Trafficking.* Peace Institute, Ljubljana.

Collinson, S. 1996. *Shore to shore: The politics of migration in Euro-Maghreb relations.* Royal Institute of International Affairs, London.

Davis, D. K. (2006). "Neoliberalism, environmentalism, and agricultural restructuring in Morocco." In *The Geographical Journal*, Vol. 172(2) June 2006.

Human Rights Watch. (2008). *Morocco: Investigate Migrant Deaths at Sea.* <http://www.hrw.org/english/docs/2008/05/09/morocc18784.htm> (19 Jan. 2009).

Kandela, P. (2000). "Women's Rights, a tourist boom and the power of khat in Yemen." *The Lancet*, 355, 1437.

Limanowska, B. (2005). "The victim perspective—a neglected dimension" in Sector project against trafficking (eds.) *Challenging trafficking in persons: theoretical debate and practical approaches.* Nomos, Baden-Baden.

Pajnic, M. (2004). "Trafficked women in media representations," in S.Z. Zimic (ed) *Women and Trafficking.* Peace Institute, Ljubljana.

Pearson, E. (2005). "Historical development of trafficking," in Sector project against trafficking (eds.) *Challenging trafficking in persons: theoretical debate and practical approaches.* Nomos, Baden-Baden.

Sater, J. (2007). "Changing politics from below? Women parliamentarians in Morocco." *Democratization*, 14(4) August 2007.

Venema, B. (2004). "A permissive zone for prostitution in the Middle Atlas of Morocco." *Ethnology*, Winter 2004, 43(1).

White, G. (2007). "The Maghreb's subordinator position in the World's Political Economy." In *Middle East Policy*, 15(4).

Zimic, S.Z. 2004. "Sex trafficking: the state, security, criminality, morality, and the victim" in S.Z. Zimic (ed) *Women and Trafficking.* Peace Institute, Ljubljana.

9

Addicted to Cheap Labor: The Gulf States, the Near East, and Trafficking

Brian E. Crim

They placed us in a hotel. They had special interest in young virgins. They were selling them at enormous prices to rich Arab sheiks for one night, after which they were working with clients like ordinary girls. We received only a fraction of what the sheiks gave to the pimp. In some cases the girls received some special presents from the sheiks. My friend who was 13 was taken to a wealthy man. In the end the man asked her what she wanted from him as a present. The girl asked for two sacks of flour. (Parrot and Cummings, 2008, 14–15)

—Shahnara (United Arab Emirates),

THE DISTURBING ACCOUNT BY SHAHNARA, a victim of sex trafficking in the wealthy Gulf state of the United Arab Emirates (UAE), dramatizes the plight of women and children forced into the sex trade in a region where human trafficking of all kinds is an accepted and entrenched part of the economy and social structure. While the vast majority of human traffickers are men, the United Nations (UN) estimates that women are two-thirds of their victims and girls represent thirteen percent (UNODC, 2009). Of the approximately 29 million people enslaved worldwide, only 4 percent are considered sex slaves. However, this 4 percent generates approximately 40 percent of all profits derived from forced labor (Kara, 2008). Global sex trafficking thrives because the potential profits are enormous, and many nations are unable or unwilling to devote sufficient resources to eradicating the practice. The numbers of women and girls entering the trade each year range from

1.2 million to four million (Dunlop, 2008). Despite such wildly divergent estimates, it is undeniable that the sex trade is extremely profitable and expanding rapidly because of accelerated globalization: sex trafficking accounts for approximately US$12 billion annually, making it only slightly less profitable than human trafficking and narcotics (Dickenson, 2006).

Without sufficient law enforcement, border security, and a cultural sensitivity to the problem of sex trafficking, no region can improve its record on this issue. Unfortunately, the Near East, specifically the Gulf region, is ill equipped and often unwilling to address sex trafficking in a substantive manner. The dynamics of sex trafficking in the Near East can best be understood by applying the Core-Dependency model familiar to political economists and historians of imperialism. In this model, core nations with advanced economies exploit the labor and natural resources of less developed areas, creating a relationship of dependency between poorer regions and the core nations. In the Near East, the Gulf States act as the core and the surrounding states like Egypt, Syria, the Palestinian territories, Iran and Iraq represents the periphery. The periphery states and other developing states outside of the region, send large numbers of migrant workers to the Gulf to fulfill its demand for construction and domestic labor.

The Core: The Gulf States and Human Trafficking

The Gulf region has one of the largest expatriate workforces in the world. Women represent 30 percent of the approximately 10 million migrant workers in the Near East. A significant number of these women are forced to become sex workers and suffer sexual abuse while working as domestic laborers. Anti-Slavery International notes that in the Gulf states, "[f]oreign female domestic workers sometimes outnumber the household members" (2006, 5). The enormous oil profits flowing into the Gulf region beginning in the 1970s sparked a dramatic increase in immigration from the poorer regions of the Near East and Asia. While the Gulf States required both skilled and unskilled labor to manage the new economy, migrant women from Bangladesh, Thailand, the Philippines and Indonesia filled the incredible demand for domestic workers. The new wealth pouring into the Gulf states made employing a foreign domestic worker, such as a maid or nanny, an important status symbol and a crucial part of "middle class identity" (Anti-Slavery International, 2006, 19). The situation for the workers themselves is precarious since these women constitute "informal labor" and remain an invisible part of the workforce in the Gulf region. Under these circumstances, foreign domestic workers in states like Saudi Arabia are systematically abused and exploited (Human

Rights Watch, 2008). Even the Saudi Minister of Labor acknowledged the problems inherent in relying on foreign labor: "I cannot monitor eight million households. There is not anywhere else in the world like this, our society is addicted to cheap labor and workers are desperate to come here" (93). While most women and girls ensnared in the global sex trafficking ring are far from willing participants, it is attitudes like these that explain why sex trafficking continues to flourish in the Gulf states and the surrounding region.

According to the Gulf Cooperation Council (GCC), the Near East is both a transit zone and destination zone for human trafficking from Asia, Eastern Europe and the CIS states and several African countries. The largest numbers of trafficked persons come from Bangladesh and Afghanistan, but women and girls forced into the sex trade also come from Europe, Africa and Asia. In the UAE, home to the burgeoning pleasure destination of Dubai, the U.S. State Department estimates that 10,000 women from Africa, Eastern Europe, South and East Asia, Iran, Iraq and Morocco "may be victims of sex trafficking" (Leghari, 2007, 112). Some of the illegal migrants pass through the system undetected and with ease many domestic workers are forced into the sex trade. After being lured to the Gulf by false promises of high-paying jobs as domestic workers, some women's papers are confiscated and fall under the control of traffickers, some of whom are in organized gangs. These women are soon forced to earn money for their captors in makeshift brothels and often face physical abuse. Government officials do not regulate domestic workers sufficiently because they fall under the umbrella of the *Kafala* system of hospitality that delineates a sponsor's obligation to foreign guest workers, including fair treatment and protection. In practice, *Kafala* results in "a system of structural dependence of the migrant worker on her/his employer" (Anti-Slavery International, 2006, 5). In Dubai the trafficking network is so entrenched that new arrivals receive forged passports and visas in the airport before reaching their final destination. This scenario indicates that airline personnel, security, and immigration officials are all involved in human trafficking (Leghari, 2007, 100–101). With an economy largely dependent on migrant labor, what is the UAE or any other Gulf state's incentive to crack down on these illegal practices?

The U.S. State Department's annual Trafficking in Persons Report (TIP) has a tier system that judges countries according to their compliance to the Victims of Trafficking and Violence Protection Act (2000). The congressional act officially targets sex trafficking and modern forms of slavery by requiring countries that receive U.S. foreign aid to comply with the legal provisions in the act, specifically prosecuting trafficking crimes and providing services for victims. Tier 1 nations are fully compliant; Tier 2 nations and those on the Tier 2 Watch List do not fully comply, but are making efforts to do so; Tier 3 nations are not compliant and make no significant efforts to do so. Of the seven Gulf states: four are listed as Tier 3 nations (Kuwait, Oman, Qatar, and Saudi Arabia), Bahrain is a Tier 2 Watch List country, while the UAE and Yemen are Tier 2. The UAE moved from a Tier 3 to a Tier 2 designation in 2008 after passing concrete efforts to reduce human trafficking, specifically the number of sex workers in Dubai (TIP, 2008).

Kuwait is a destination and transit country for migrants impressed into forced labor and sexual exploitation. In particular, female domestic workers are in danger of being forced into prostitution after fleeing abusive households. Kuwait is home to several disreputable labor agencies that send low-skilled labor to Iraq as well as to organized gangs involved in the sex trade. In addition, the TIP reports that Kuwaiti nationals engage in "sex tourism" by traveling to other parts of the Near East and Southeast Asia. Despite passing a series of laws designed to punish offenders and strengthen immigration measures, Kuwait is not proactive in prosecuting cases. Worse, Kuwait, like many Gulf States, punishes the victims of sex trafficking through deportation and imprisonment more often than the sex traffickers themselves.

Oman is also a destination and transit country for migrants from within other states in the Near East. Specifically, it is a destination country for women from Asia, Eastern Europe, and North Africa who are often victims of commercial sexual exploitation. Many Pakistani nationals, both willingly and unwillingly, travel to Oman before being smuggled to other Gulf locations (Leghari, 2007). Oman does not prosecute trafficking offenses or make any effort to either identify or protect victims aside from symbolic education measures and a labor abuse hotline. There is a chronic problem in Oman with underreporting of specifically sex trafficking cases, because many victims fear detention or deportation to even worse destinations (TIP, 2008). *Qatar* is a destination for migrants slated for involuntary servitude as well as for prostitutes from Asia, North Africa, and other parts of the Near East. Like Oman, Qatar has an extremely poor law enforcement record and devotes minimal resources to prevention and victim identification or other services.

The Kingdom of Saudi Arabia's lengthy and porous borders makes it vulnerable to countless illicit border crossings, specifically near Iraq and Yemen (Leghari, 2007, 124). In addition, Saudi Arabia is one of the largest destination countries for low-skilled labor and domestic servants from around the globe. Additionally, according to the TIP, women from Yemen, Morocco, Pakistan, Nigeria, Ethiopia, Tajikistan, and Thailand are trafficked to Saudi Arabia for commercial sexual exploitation. Some women in Saudi Arabia were reportedly kidnapped and forced into the sex trade after fleeing corrupt employers. With the *Kafala* system replacing legitimate legal protection for workers, foreign women, especially Asian domestic workers in many Saudi households are at the mercy of their employers and suffer physical and sexual abuse. The Saudi Minister of Social Affairs admitted the problem, "Contracts are not clear, agents in KSA [Saudi Arabia] are lousy and dishonest.... Some employers treat domestic workers like slaves, some treat them like members of their families" (Human Rights Watch, 2008, 22).

Considered the "Las Vegas of the Middle East," the UAE, specifically Dubai, is a natural hub for human trafficking and remains a destination and transit country for illegal labor and prostitution. While climbing to Tier 2 status in 2008, women from Central Asia, Eastern Europe, Africa, South Asia and Southeast Asia fill the brothels of Dubai. The TIP reports that women are often recruited to fill legitimate jobs under false pretenses before being coerced into the sex trade or domestic servitude. The UAE earned its ascent to the Tier 2 category by improving law enforcement and hiring hundreds of labor inspectors trained to identify trafficking violations. However, like the other Gulf States, the UAE continues to criminalize victims of sex trafficking by assuming they are willing participants. In addition, the UAE is reluctant to initiate an effective public awareness campaign that highlights the extent of the trafficking problem.

The other Tier 2 Gulf state of Yemen is a source country for unskilled labor, children forced into beggary, and women entering the sex trade. The TIP maintains that many Yemeni women are trafficked internally or to Saudi Arabia for sexual exploitation. An impoverished nation, Yemen suffers from a growing population of street children who are vulnerable to abuse. However, the government has recognized the problem, opening a shelter for child victims in addition to criminalizing child prostitution. The Gulf is comprised of mostly wealthy states that rely on unskilled labor from other areas of the Near East and the poorer regions of the world, a dynamic that allows for near limitless opportunities for sex traffickers. This economic situation, combined with woefully inadequate criminal penalties and protections services explains why most of the Gulf States are in the Tier 3 category.

The Periphery: The Near East and Human Trafficking

The poorer states in the Near East, not including Israel, feed the Gulf states with cheap labor and victims for commercial sexual exploitation. Iran and Syria are Tier 3 nations; Egypt and Jordan are currently on the Tier 2 Watch List; Israel and Lebanon occupy Tier 2 positions. However, the most problematic state in the region is Iraq. The TIP is not yet ready to assess Iraq according to the Tier system because Iraq is still in transition, but the situation is dire for men, women, and children in every category of human trafficking. The TIP maintains that children are specifically targeted for sexual exploitation and trafficked within the country by criminal gangs and even private orphanages. The Organization of Women's Freedom reports that 3500 women have gone missing from Iraq since the occupation (IRIN, 2006). In response, several governments banned travel of their nationals to Iraq for fear of being trafficked. Traffickers working out of Syria and the UAE are operating with impunity and will continue do so for the foreseeable future unless the international community devotes sufficient resources on the ground and a stable Iraqi government institutes its own anti-trafficking measures.

Syria is a Tier 3 nation in part because of the freedom traffickers enjoy along the Iraqi border, but Syria is also a destination and transit country for women and children involved in forced labor and sexual exploitation. Aside from Iraqi refugees, women from Somalia, Russia, Central Asia and Eastern Europe are forced into prostitution and dance clubs. The TIP also suggests that Syria is a destination for sex tourism for others parts of the Near East. A protection officer with the UNCHR in Damascus stated that it is impossible to comprehend the scope of the trafficking problem from Iraq to Syria because "[i]t is something that has been quiet because people are afraid to talk about it" (IRIN, 2006). Syria is not actively prosecuting trafficking crimes despite sufficient laws on the books. Like many Tier 3 nations, the absence of law is not the issue so much as the unwillingness to act. Worse, Syria is more likely to arrest the victims of trafficking and subject them to further abuse than to prosecute the traffickers. Iran, the last Tier 3 nation in the Near East, is a source, transit and destination country for women and children forced into servitude and the sex trade. Iranian women are trafficked internally because of forced marriages or debt settlement and trafficked externally to other parts of the Near East and Europe for sexual exploitation. The TIP claims that the Iranian government imprisons, beats, and even executes female victims of trafficking.

Egypt has been a Tier 2 Watch List state for three years running primarily because it fails to provide evidence that the government investigates and prosecutes trafficking crimes despite having legislation on the books. Egypt is a transit country for women from Russia, Central Asia and Eastern Europe destined for sexual exploitation and domestic servitude in Israel. Cairo is plagued with an estimated one million "street children" who are extremely vulnerable to sexual abuse and prostitution. The TIP reports that wealthy Gulf citizens travel to Egypt to purchase "temporary marriages" with underage girls from willing parents and corrupt marriage brokers. Egypt may also host sex tourists from around the world.

Jordan too is on the Watch List for failing to combat trafficking or to empower law enforcement to prosecute cases related to forced labor and the exploitation of domestic workers. Jordan is a transit and destination country for men and women from various parts of Asia impressed into forced labor. As a nation bordering Iraq, traffickers actively lure unskilled workers with false promises and send them to unregulated worksites in Iraq. The TIP also labels Jordan a destination country for prostitutes from Eastern Europe and North Africa. The Philippine government banned its female citizens traveling to Jordan for employment until Jordan addresses the issue of domestic worker abuse. Inadequate law enforcement and selective or minimal prosecution of trafficking offenses ensures that both Egypt and Jordan will remain on the Watch List for the immediate future.

The Tier 2 nations in the Near East are Lebanon and Israel. Lebanon is a destination country for trafficked women from Asia and Africa slated for domestic work as well as for Eastern European and Syrian women involved in the sex trade (Anti-Slavery International, 2006). Foreign women are often subject to threats and assault, to having their movements restricted, and passports confiscated by traffickers or employers—all familiar tactics employed against women lured to a state under false pretenses. The TIP maintains that children are also trafficked within the country for labor and sexual exploitation. Israel is a destination country for men and women trafficked for labor and prostitution. Israel attracts low-skilled workers to different sectors of its economy, but workers must pay recruitment fees in the thousands of dollars. This debt makes workers vulnerable to exploitation and abuse. Israel continues to struggle with a significant prostitution problem involving women from Russia, Eastern Europe, Central and Southeast Asia, and China. The TIP notes Israeli women are trafficked internally and possibly abroad to Canada, Ireland and Britain. Despite efforts to expedite prosecution of trafficking cases and to increase victim protection services, these measures still fall below the minimum standards for eliminating trafficking.

Conclusion

The Gulf States are flush with financial resources, but lack the will to substantively crack down on human trafficking in all of its forms, specifically sexual exploitation. The UN, the U.S. State Department, and nongovernmental organizations recognize that most countries in the Near East have passed legislation criminalizing trafficking, but none are Tier 1 states. The Gulf is truly "addicted to cheap labor" and domestic workers are susceptible to sexual abuse. Dubai continues to attract thousands of sex workers, many of whom are forced into prostitution, and the brothels in nations like Israel, Lebanon, Egypt and Jordan are filled with women ensnared in the global sex trafficking ring. Siddarth Kara, a noted scholar on the subject of slavery and trafficking, recommends several international and state-specific measures to address sex trafficking. His most dramatic proposal is an international slavery and trafficking inspection force that operates like UN weapons inspectors, along with community vigilance committees that are sensitized to the issue and can recognize trafficking in their own communities (Kara and Stewart, 2009). The Near East must simply increase criminal penalties and most importantly, launch a coordinated public awareness campaign that stresses the horrors and abuses integral to trafficking. A spokesman for Qatar, which is beginning to teach the issue in schools, stated, "The issue of human trafficking must figure in modern curriculums in order to raise awareness and ensure a secure future for our societies." (humantrafficking.org, 2008) Encouraging words to be sure, but so far Near Eastern states are more focused on rhetoric than action.

References

Anti-Slavery International. (2006). *Trafficking in Women, Forced Labour and Domestic Work in the Context of the Middle East and Gulf Region.*

Dickenson, D. (2006). "Philosophical Assumptions and Presumptions about Trafficking for Prostitution," in Christien L. van den Anker and Jeroen Doomernik (eds) *Trafficking and Women's Rights.* New York: Palgrave Macmillan.

Dunlop, K. 2008. "Human Security, Sex Trafficking and Deep Structural Explanations." *Human Security Journal,* 6 (Spring).

Human Rights Watch. (2008). *"As If I Am Not Human:" Abuses against Asian Domestic Workers in Saudi Arabia.*

Humantrafficking.org. (2008). "Arab Schools Urged to Teach Ills of Human Trafficking." <Humantrafficking.org/updates/792> (8 July 2009).

IRIN: UN Office for the Coordination of Humanitarian Affairs. (2006). "Sex traffickers target women in war-torn Iraq." October 26, 2006. www.irinnews.org/report.aspx?reportid=61903 (8 July 2009).

Kara, S. (2008). *Sex Trafficking: Inside the Business of Modern Slavery.* NY: Columbia University.

Leghari, F. (2007). *Narcotics and Human Trafficking to the GCC States.* Gulf Research Center, Dubai.

Madslien, J. (2005). "Sex trade's reliance on forced labor." BBC. <news.bbc.co.uk/1/hi/business/4532617.stm> (18 July 2009).

Parrot, A., and Cummings, N. (2008). *Sexual Enslavement of Girls and Women Worldwide.* Westport, CT: Praeger.

U.S. Department of State. (2008, June). *Trafficking in Persons.* Report. Washington, DC: Office to Combat and Monitor Trafficking in Persons.

V

SOUTH ASIA

Kimberly A. McCabe and Sabita Manian

I N SOUTH AND CENTRAL ASIA, THE CULTURAL aspects of servitude and the re-
pression of women facilitate the criminal activity of sex trafficking. International trafficking, especially the sex trafficking of children within Asia, occupies one of the largest segments of the global trade of people (Mirkinson,
1997). This section provides two chapters—one on India and the other on
Afghanistan—to provide specific explanations to the question of why is sex
trafficking so prevalent in South and Central Asia.

Many of the countries in Central and South Asia serve as source countries
for victims of sex trafficking. As suggested, the key characteristics of source
countries include most of the population suffering from extreme poverty and
women are treated as essentially the property of their fathers, brothers, or
husbands. Both of the countries highlighted in this section exist with those
two characteristics.

In India, it is estimated that millions of people are trafficked on an annual
basis. Approximately 25 percent of India's population lives below the poverty
line and over one-half of the population are female. Traffickers are aware of
those conditions in India and utilize these conditions to their advantage (Mc-
Cabe, 2008). In addition, government officials suggest that 90 percent of India's trafficking is internal (Banerjee, 2006). Because of India's historical reliance on slavery, sex trafficking is almost natural.

Specifically, India was built with slave labor. At one time, young girls were
dedicated to serving the priest of the temples both in terms of labor and sex.
Debt servitude has also existed for centuries in India along with the caste sys-

tem of servants and royalty. India is a growing destination for sex tourists from Europe and the United States. Law enforcement efforts to reduce sex trafficking continue to be uncoordinated with weak networks of communications among the various police agencies. Corruption of government authorities continues to exist and little in terms of sensitivity training for police in working with victims exists. Finally, in India, victims of sex trafficking are often punished for prostitution. Therefore, sex trafficking is a logical outcome from the social, economic, and historical conditions of India; add the element of organized crime and sex trafficking flourishes.

Afghanistan exists as a country with nearly three decades of armed conflict and an extremely weak governmental infrastructure. In countries such as Afghanistan, the drug trade continues and is essentially controlled by organized crime. As the drug trade and the production of opium have existed for decades, the incorporation of sex trafficking into an already successfully existing crime structure seems reasonable. Without adopting comprehensive anti-trafficking legislation and without cooperation from border countries, there will be little in terms of governmental deterrence to reduce sex trafficking. With law enforcement either a part of the drug trafficking organization or pressed by limited financial resources to maintain law and social order among a drug cartel, efforts to reduce sex trafficking are rare.

From 2003 to 2006, only one piece of legislation was` enacted in an attempt to control sex trafficking throughout South and Central Asia. Women and children in India and Afghanistan are kidnapped, deceived, or sold for sex trafficking. Judiciary practices are conflicted by a mixture of legal codes and customary law which often leave victims of sex trafficking at risk for legal punishments if they are discovered by law enforcement. Relationships between government officials and representatives from nongovernment organizations are often strained and communication efforts unreliable. Therefore, sex trafficking continues to increase. The two chapters in this section discuss not only the growing prevalence of sex trafficking in the region, but also the countries' inattention to the problem.

References

Banerjee, U. (2006). "Migration and Trafficking of Women and Children. A Brief Review of Some Effective Models in India and Thailand." In K. Beeks and D. Amir (eds.) *Trafficking and the Global Sex Trafficking.* Lanham, MD: Lexington.

McCabe, K. (2008). *The Trafficking of Persons: National and International Responses.* NY: Peter Lang.

Mirkinson, J. (1997). "The Global Trade in Women." *Earth Island Journal,* 13(1), 30–31.

10

Trafficking in India

Arvind Verma

O F THE 27 MILLION ESTIMATED "slaves" [people living in bondage] world-wide, approximately 18 million of them are in India (Bales, 2005). The nation has also acquired a notorious reputation for facilitating the trafficking of women from neighboring countries of Nepal and Bangladesh. India is reportedly a major sending, receiving and transit nation "for the purposes of forced labor and commercial sexual exploitation" (TIP, 2008). While the usual trafficking of women and young girls for commercial sexual exploitation (CSE) is well known, the trafficking of children for purposes of forced labor in factories, agriculture, and domestic help and for illegal activities is equally rampant. Moreover, a system of forced labor is another phenomenon through which millions of families have been virtually enslaved as "bonded labor" forced to work at pittance for small loans that they cannot repay. Receiving children from Bangladesh and Nepal and sending women and children to Middle Eastern nations is a common occurrence (Sleightholme and Sinha, 1997). The major proportion of women and children are trafficked from four states within India: Andhra Pradesh, Karnataka, West Bengal and Tamil Nadu and among the trafficked persons, majority of them are girls lured at a very young age.

While most of the trafficking takes place for purposes of CSE, children are also taken away or virtually sold by their parents to work domestically as indentured labor in small factories, homes and shops. A large proportion, especially young boys, also fall prey to sex tourists from Europe and North America (including the United States) because of lenient laws and abundant child prostitutes (Bedi, 1996; *The Indian Express,* 1997). Trafficking and prostitution are also related to the growing epidemic of HIV-Aids virus with an estimated 5.1 million Indians currently infected with the virus. Despite efforts by the government and NGOs, HIV prevalence among female sex workers has not fallen below 52 percent since 2000 (National Aids Control Organization, 2004). Abject poverty, widespread illiteracy and lax legal protection are some of the causes that lie behind this gruesome situation. Further, a majority of the victims are from broken poor families and socially weaker sections of society.

This chapter will first describe the human trafficking situation in the country and then present the efforts of the state, particularly the police to combat this problem. Efforts of international agencies that assist Indian authorities in preventing human trafficking will also be examined. Finally, the impact of the government's efforts and some of their innovative practices to address this scourge will be assessed.

Historical Roots of Trafficking in India

Trafficking in India has roots in three forms of social practices that have continued for three millennia. Slavery was fairly common in ancient India and is recorded in many historical texts. The enslavement of defeated population by the victorious kings and their armies was an acceptable practice in the region as late as the seventeenth century. Rulers maintained large harems that were populated by young women and boys kidnapped from all parts of the kingdom. The nobility too indulged in this form of sexual exploitation that was considered a right of the aristocracy. Slave markets existed in major Indian cities and continued until the nineteenth century when European colonial powers made profits from such trade. Despite the abolition of slavery in Britain in 1843, at the end of the nineteenth century there were reports of female family members being sold to pay off debts (*The New York Times,* 1873).

Another ancient practice that has allegedly promoted human bondage is the system of "Devadasi" that has existed for more than two thousand years. As a *devadasi,* or servant of god, young girls were dedicated at puberty to the goddess Yellamma. European missionaries denounced these artistic performances as vulgar and castigated the women (for maintaining sexual relations outside the formal marriage system) as prostitutes (Chawla, 2008). The British abolished this system resulting in pushing the practice underground and becoming associated with the flesh trade. Today there are still around fifty thousand *devadasis* in the country and most of them are not practicing the ancient customs as institutional support has declined (Reddy, 2002). Most have been targeted by pimps who trick them into the red light districts of major Indian cities (Thorold, 2002). The government and many NGOs have initiated efforts to assist these women in finding alternate employment (Menon, 2007).

Another form of practice known as "begar" has been instrumental in pushing people into debt servitude in India. Evolved as a creditor debtor relationship over centuries this affects a large number of rural and commercial transactions. A person unable to pay the debt, "mortgages" his family, which constitutes a bonded labor relationship that continues till the debt is paid (Finn, 2008). These practices have led to the trafficking of children and females who are forced to work in brick kilns, carpet weaving factories, agricultural laborers and bonded in servitude. Child labor, arising from family debt problems in particular has become widespread with almost 200 million children working long hours in unhealthy, physically daunting and hazardous conditions and are vulnerable to sexual exploitation, with a large proportion slaving as bonded laborers (Sooryamoorthy, 1998).

Even though the situation in India remains alarming, trafficking of children and girls from lower socioeconomic background is showing a declining trend. There are two specific laws that criminalize human trafficking viz.: (i) Immoral Trafficking (Prevention) Act 1956; and (ii) Child Marriage Restraint Act, 1929. According to the National Crime Records Bureau (2008), the Indian police record trafficking cases under the Indian Penal Code is as follows:

(i) Procuring minor girls for immoral purposes (366-A IPC)
(ii) Importation of girls (previously called "Eve-Teasing," 366-B IPC)
(iii) Selling of girls for prostitution (372 IPC)
(iv) Buying of girls for prostitution (373 IPC)

The regional breakup of these data suggest that the worst affected provinces are Tamil Nadu, Karnataka and Andhra Pradesh in southern India where the Devadasi system was prevalent and so perhaps that tradition has had an im-

TABLE 10.1
Cases of Child Exploitation by Penal Code (2002–2006)

Crime Head	2002	2003	2004	2005	2006
366A IPC	124	171	205	145	231
366B-IPC	76	46	89	149	67
372 IPC	5	36	19	50	123
373 IPC	9	24	21	28	35
Imm Tr Act 1956	6598	5510	5748	5908	4541
Child Marr Res Act 1929	113	63	93	122	99
Total	6925	5850	6175	6402	5096

Source: National Crime Records Bureau, 2008

pact upon the present trafficking situation. The destinations of most of the girls trafficked in the country are Mumbai, Delhi, Kolkata and other major metropolitan cities for CSE. A problem with this data is that Indian police's record-keeping is poor and there are several organizational problems in documenting complaints brought by the citizens. Under the law, a citizen complaint of a cognizable crime must be registered and all crime statistics are derived from this registration. Unfortunately, the police exercise considerable prerogative in applying this section and many citizen complaints are filed in other ways. For instance, complaints of trafficking are largely recorded as "missing person" reports which do not come under the scrutiny of supervisory officers and the courts. Ironically, the UN guidelines endorsed by India and the United States define trafficking in a more comprehensive manner. Trafficking is defined as a criminal process involving transportation and or receiving of human beings with means that are fraudulent or deceitful and for the purposes of servitude, forced labor and or sexual exploitation. Undoubtedly, adopting this definition will display different statistics and a much larger number of people victimized by traffickers than reported by the National Crime Records Bureau.

Moreover, a research report (Nigam, 2008) pointed out that the police agencies accord low priority to human trafficking issues and most officers seem insensitive to the gravity of the problems. Indeed, many times the trafficked women themselves are arrested for soliciting or harassed in other ways. The police investigation rarely goes beyond the place where the victim is rescued and thus the perpetrators and traffickers escape penalization. Even though, there is clear evidence of organized gangs operating in this crime and involving offenders like recruiters, transporters, traffickers, exploiters and conspirators, the police seldom investigate their links. Police agencies fail to coordinate with other agencies across their state boundaries and are disinclined to work with NGOs who understand the situation better. Finally, there is a lack of effort towards rehabilitation that prevents victims from being trafficked again.

The U.S. State Department's annual TIP report (2008) places India as a Tier 2 nation for the fifth year in succession. Traffickers adopt fraudulent recruitment practices that trap unsuspecting people directly into situations of forced labor, including debt bondage. In some other cases high debts incurred to pay recruitment fees leave them vulnerable to exploitation in the destination countries. Moreover, abandoned in distant places these people are subjected to conditions of involuntary servitude, nonpayment of wages, restrictions on movement, unlawful withholding of passports, and physical or sexual abuse (TIP, 2008). Disturbingly, there are reports of children being forced to function as armed combatants by some terrorist groups and even the government agencies (Dixit, 2007). The Asian Center for Human Rights (ACHR) also reported that one local government (in Chattisgarh) recruited children as Special Police Officers (SPOs) to combat the left-wing *naxal* groups and found in January 2007 "continued practice of recruitment of underaged children as SPOs" (2006: 8).

Human trafficking has become an organized crime in the country generating US$8 million (Global Citizens Trust, 2008). According to Human Rights Watch (1995) hundreds of thousands, and probably more than a million women and children are employed in Indian brothels. There are well documented trafficking routes within South Asia, from Bangladesh, Nepal and Pakistan to India, and widely within India, particularly to the cities of Kolkata and Mumbai where they are taken on the false pretext of marriage or for providing employment (Coomaraswamy, 2000). Moreover, most of the girls are either sold to traffickers by poor parents or tricked into fraudulent marriages from where they are transported to the brothels of Mumbai, Kolkata, Bangalore and other major cities. A good number are tricked by traffickers on the promise of employment in urban areas only to find themselves in brothels. These girl children are locked up for days, starved, beaten, and tortured until they learn how to service up to 25 clients a day. Some girls go through "training" before being initiated into prostitution, which can include constant exposure to pornographic films, tutorials, and repeated rapes (Wadhwa, 1998). Friedman (1996) states that prostitution in Bombay generates millions of dollars a year in revenue but most of the money is cornered by the pimps and brothel owners while the prostitutes barely earn $2 a day. Unfortunately, a large proportion of prostituted women in Bombay's red-light district areas are also infected with STD and AIDS (CATW, 2008) which is creating another catastrophe in the country.

Preventive Measures

There are many efforts initiated by the Indian government to deal with this problem. The *Protocol to Prevent, Suppress and Punish Trafficking in Persons,* especially women and children, supplementing the *UN Convention against Transnational Organized Crime* (Trafficking Protocol) was signed by the Government of India in 2002. The National Human Rights Commission (2008) has stated that this is a huge step forward as it not only prevents and protects the victims of trafficking but also punishes the traffickers.

The Constitution of India forbids trafficking in "human beings and *begar* and other similar forms of forced labor" and further prohibits employment of children below 14 years of age in factories, mines or other hazardous employment. The commitment to curb human trafficking is also reflected in various legislations and policy documents (e.g., the Karnataka *Devdasi* Prohibition of Dedication Act, 1982; Child Labour Prohibition and Regulation Act, 1986; Andhra Pradesh *Devdasi* Prohibiting Dedication Act, 1989) and other collateral laws having relevance to trafficking. The Supreme Court through its public interest litigation process (Verma, 2001) forced the government to form a Committee to look into the problems of CSE and trafficking of women and children and of children of trafficked victims and to evolve suitable schemes to deal with the problem. Forced by the courts, public outcry, and media reports the Indian government drew up a National Plan of Action to Combat Trafficking and Commercial Sexual Exploitation of Women and Children in 1998. Furthermore, the Ministry of Women and Child Development, in collaboration with UNICEF, has developed protocols on the rescue and rehabilitation of child victims trafficked for CSE and has developed three manuals that seek to establish norms in dealing with the problem of trafficking in the country (http://wcd.nic.in/).

A notable effort has been made by the UN office of Drugs and Crime [UNODC]–India to raise awareness of police, civil and judicial officers about trafficking. These efforts led to the creation of Integrated Anti–Human Trafficking Units [IAHTU] at the provincial levels consisting of police, prosecutors, NGOs, labor, health and welfare representatives and concerned citizens. A senior police officer heads the unit and oversees intelligence collection, maintenance of databases of known traffickers, expeditious prosecution, care for victims through collaboration with NGOs, preventative actions such as policing vulnerable areas and overseeing public transport terminals to intervene in trafficking situations. Five states have established such units and more are to follow. The UNODC has also assisted in the development of training modules, standard operating procedures, handbooks and compendium of best practices to strengthen the IAHTUs and police forces. Training manual for public prosecutors, protocol for victim care and assistance and even a manual for psychosocial intervention, keeping human rights issues in perspective for police and prosecutors are other useful documents developed by this body. A major public awareness initiative was launched in April 2006 through short films (including the endorsement of Bollywood stars) screened nationally that emphasizes the prevention of trafficking, prosecution of offenders and protection of victims (UNODC, 2008).

The UNODC also provided the IAHTUs with material resources like computers, special vehicles and surveillance equipment to enhance their capacity. The IAHTU is part of a program for police training and capacity building undertaken by the UNODC in partnership with the government and financially supported by the US $2.5 million from Washington (UNODC, 2007).

During the period between January and September 2007, a total of 96 operations were launched that helped rescue 716 women including 108 minor girls. A total of 1020 traffickers and 332 "customers" were arrested while 466 criminal cases were registered against them (Nigam, 2008). In Andhra Pradesh, two of these offenders were also convicted for child trafficking which was a first for the state. The UNODC is in the process of assisting other state governments to establish such special units for anti-trafficking work. While police undertake rescue operations along with NGOs, other government departments immediately move in, to provide interim relief to the victims. The NGOs then take over post-rescue care and attention in association with the government agencies concerned.

An innovative preventive action has been launched in eastern India where authorities have teamed up with prostitutes in West Bengal's Sonagachhi area, one of Asia's largest red-light districts, to combat trafficking. In 2008 alone a sex workers' organization rescued more than 550 women and girls from brothels and from traffickers (Majumdar, 2008). These results have helped differentiate between sex workers and those women trafficked for sexual exploitation. Regarding the system of bonded labor, various state governments have undertaken special efforts to rescue children forced into labor: during the reporting period, raids throughout the country yielded 333 children rescued and five individuals arrested (TIP, 2008).

Despite these recent and strong efforts the problems of trafficking in the country remain acute. The TIP report castigates the Indian government for its failures to prevent trafficking and to punish the offenders involved in this criminal activity. A singular failure has been the inability to successfully prosecute traffickers and the rate of conviction for kidnapping and abduction of women is abysmally small. In 2006, conviction was achieved in only 538 cases of kidnapping and abduction out of 10492 set for trial. For the offense of buying girls for CSE only 3 cases (out of 72) resulted in convictions (National Crime Records Bureau, 2008). Despite the estimated millions of bonded laborers in India, only 19 suspects were arrested for trafficking for bonded labor during the reporting period (TIP, 2008). Regardless of a law banning child labor there is no enforcement of it; even as poverty, unemployment and illiteracy continue to be the most important factors contributing to it. Given the complex socioeconomic dimensions of the problem, improvement in the working conditions of unorganized industrial sectors and education of vulnerable families is crucial to the elimination of child labor.

Unfortunately, the challenges before the Indian state to accelerate economic development and upliftment of the masses are formidable. Despite the recent economic revival and visible growth in the middle class the majority of the population lives in abject poverty: ranked 55th amongst

102 developing countries on the Human Poverty Index mark, India has an adult literacy rate of 39 percent (UNDP, 2006), an infant mortality rate of 57 per thousand live births (UNICEF, 2008), and about 26 percent of India's population is officially classed as poor—that is people getting less than the minimum number of calories regarded as necessary for survival (Malhotra, 2008). Although the Indian government immediately defended its efforts in tackling human trafficking (a day after the 2008 TIP report was released), the challenges facing the nation in alleviating poverty remain daunting; it seems unlikely that child labor, bonded labor and sex trafficking will end soon.

References

Asian Center for Human Rights. (2007). Naxal Conflict in 2006. New Delhi. <www.achrweb.org/reports/india/naxal0107.pdf> (5 March 2009).

Bakhry, S. (2005). "Designing and implementing an action research project on trafficking: a perspective from NHRC India." Paper presented at the Regional Workshop on Trafficking and National Human Rights Institutions. Australia, 20–23 November.

Bales, K. (2005). *Understanding Global Slavery*. Berkeley: University of California Press.

Bedi, R. (1996). "Bid to protect children as sex tourism spreads" *News–Scan international*, 19(3).

Chawla, A. (2008). *Devadasis: Sinners or Sinned Against* <SamarthBharat.com>

Coalition against Trafficking in Women [CATW]. (2008). *Trafficking in Women and Prostitution in the Asia Pacific* <http://www.catwinternational.org/factbook/india.php> (5 March 2009).

Coomaraswamy, R. (2000). "Integration of the Human Rights of Women and the Gender Perspective Violence against Women." UN Special Report on Violence against Women, Commission on Human Rights, 56th Session, February 29.

Dixit, M. (2007). India's Forgotten Children of War. *CounterCurrents.* <www.counter-currents.org/dixit051207.htm> (15 March 2009).

Finn, D. (2008) "Bonded Labor in India" in *Topical Research Digest Human Rights and Contemporary Slavery Human Rights and Human Welfare: An International Review of Books.* <http://www.du.edu/korbel/hrhw/digest/slavery/> (15 March 2009).

Friedman, R. (1996). "India's Shame: Sexual Slavery and Political Corruption Are Leading to an AIDs Catastrophe." *The Nation*, April 8.

Global Citizens Trust. (2008). "Human trafficking turning into organised crime in India" Zee News June 21. <http://www.zeenews.com/articles.asp?aid=303996&sid=NAT> (14 March 2009).

Human Rights Watch. (1995). Rape for Profit: Trafficking of Nepali Girls and Women to India's Brothels, *Human Rights Watch*, 12(5A), <http://www.hrw.org/reports/1995/India.htm> (15 March 2009).

The Indian Express. (1997). "Global laws to punish sex tourists sought by Britain and EU," November 21.

Kamat, J. (2008). Women of India: Devadasi—Servant of God [Online Essay] <http://www.kamat.com/kalranga/women/devadasi.htm> (15 March 2009).

Malhotra, K. (2008). "Poverty still grips millions in India." BBC News August 12 <http://news.bbc.co.uk/2/hi/south_asia/7556489.stm> (15 March 2009).

Majumdar, B. (2008). "India turns to prostitutes to help beat trafficking." Reuters Jan 11 <http://www.reuters.com/article/latestCrisis/idUSDEL21575> (15 March 2009).

Menon, R. (2007). India: Devadasis Uniting to End 'Dedications' India Together April 26 <http://www.indiatogether.org/2007/apr/soc-devadasi.htm> (15 March 2009).

National Aids Control Organization. (2004). An Overview of the Spread and Prevalence of HIV/AIDS in India <http://www.nacoonline.org/facts_overview.htm> (18 March 2009).

National Crime Records Bureau. (2008). *Crime in India—2006*, Faridabad, Government of India Press.

National Human Rights Commission. (2008). *NHRC's Plan of Action to Prevent and End Trafficking in Women and Children in India* <http://nhrc.nic.in/> (15 March 2009).

The New York Times. (1873). "Female slavery in India." August 21.

Nigam, S. (2008). "The Scourge of Human Trafficking in India." *Merinews* March 17 <http://www.merinews.com/catFull.jsp?articleID=131079> (18 March 2009).

Rangarajan, L. (1992). *Kautilya: The Arthashastra New Delhi.* Penguin Press.

Reddy, K. (2002). *Devadasis: Time to Review History* <www.samarthbharat.com/devadasis.htm> (18 March 2009).

Sleightholme, C., and Sinha, I. (1997). *Guilty without Trial: Women in the Sex Trade in Calcutta.* New York: Rutgers University Press.

Sooryamoorthy, R. (1998). "Child Labour in Kerala: The Work and Working Ambience in the Capital City." *Journal of Third World Studies*, 15(2): 31–52.

Spear, P. (1972). *India: A Modern History.* Ann Arbor: The University of Michigan Press.

Sulekha.com. (2007). *Nithari: The Visible and Invisible Victims* <http://nitharifacts.sulekha.com/blog/post/2007/12/nithari-the-visible-and-invisible-victims.htm> (18 March 2009).

Thorold, C. (2002). Servants of God. BBC News: June 29 <http://news.bbc.co.uk/2/hi/programmes/from_our_own_correspondent/2071612.stm> (15 March 2009).

United Nation's Children Fund 2008 The State of World's Children. (2008). <http://www.unicef.org/infobycountry/india_statistics.html> (18 March 2009).

United Nations Development Project (UNDP) (2006). *Human Development Report 2006.* <http://hdr.undp.org/en/media/hdr_tables_2006.pdf> (19 March 2009).

United Nations Office of Drugs and Crime. (2007). *Goa Acts against Human Traffickers* [Press Report] <http://www.unodc.org/india/ht_unit_goa240307.html> (18 March 2009).

———. 2008. UNODC and Bollywood Unite Against Trafficking. <http://www.unodc.org/unodc/en/frontpage/unodc-and-bollywood-unite-against-trafficking.html> (18 March 2009).

United States Department of Labor. (2008, August). 2007 Findings on the Worst Forms of Child Labor—India. <http://www.unhcr.org/refworld/docid/48caa4763d.html> (18 March 2009).

United States Department of State. (2008). 2008 Trafficking in Persons Report <http://www.state.gov/g/tip/rls/tiprpt/2008/> (18 March 2009).

Verma, A. (2001). "Taking Justice outside the Courts: Judicial Activism in India." *The Howard Journal of Criminal Justice*, 20(2): 148–165.

Wadhwa, S. (1998). "For sale: Childhood," The Outlook. <www.outlookindia.com> (18 March 2009).

11

Afghanistan and the Sex Trade

Michael A. Bush

I N THE COUNTRY OF AFGHANISTAN, particularly in the southern part of Afghanistan, it is apparent that one may purchase sex either from individuals prostituting themselves by will or by coercion. Many of those involved in the prostitution of themselves do so as their chosen occupation, however, some of those involved in prostitution of themselves are victims of sex trafficking.

Located in the regions of South and Central Asia, bordering Iran, Pakistan, Turkmenistan, Uzbekistan, and Tajikistan, is the country of Afghanistan. Of course, while Afghanistan is one of the countries heard recently in evening news reports as an area with military conflicts and innocent deaths, however, there are lesser known other aspects of the country. As reported daily by the world media, Afghanistan is a center of military conflict, insurgency, and terror. The deaths of innocent Afghans at the hands of the Taliban or other insurgents or as a result of military operations targeting those insurgents, is common. There are other troubling aspects to life in Afghanistan that draw less media scrutiny—one aspect is human trafficking. According to the CIA's 2009 World Factbook, Afghanistan has a population of approximately 33 million people with a median age of 17.6 and a life expectancy of only 44 years of age. In Afghanistan, there are high rates of infant mortality rates as well as high rates of violence. Currently, in addition to being identified as a country with one of the highest death rates in the world (19.56 per 1,000 population); Afghanistan officials report an unemployment rate of 40 percent and a population growth of 2.6 percent. The United Nations' *Committee for Refugees* states that poverty stricken Afghanistan has produced over 3.6 million new refugees. Therefore, conditions of the country of Afghanistan facilitate what sociologists and criminologists call 'social disorganization'. As revealed in Sampson and Groves' (1989) research on community structure and crime, social disorganization is directly related to crime rates and crime rates are outcomes of neighborhood ecological characteristics.

In particular, in disorganized countries mechanisms of social control are absent. In countries such as Afghanistan with institutions of social control broken, individuals and organizations can no longer perform their routine functions. Indications of social disorganization include high unemployment, high proportions of transient populations, low income levels, poverty, and high rates of migration—all of which are characteristics of Afghanistan. Those living within disorganized environments experience conflict, despair, law-violating groups or gangs, and little in terms of assistance from legal officials. In the Afghan towns, all of the characteristics of a socially disorganized area are apparent. Many individuals exist on a daily basis with the expectation of victimization.

Along with high levels of social disorganization and poverty, Afghanistan is also known as the world's largest producer of opium. The drug trade flourishes in Afghanistan because of the historical and cultural reliance on Opium production and is exacerbated by the country's current state of social disorder. Therefore, with the continuation of poor economic conditions, the drug trades continue to thrive. Of course, the drug trade is not the only form of criminal activity in Afghanistan. As criminological literature suggests, the sex trade and the drug trade often go hand in hand (Chaiken and Johnson, 1988). Smugglers transport drugs, in, out, and within a country. Human traffickers move people in, out, and within a country. In areas with little successful deterrence of the drug trade against drug trafficking, there is also little deterrence of human trafficking. What little is known about drug smugglers indicates they have strong organizational skills, established criminal and possibly political connections, and a willingness to take a risk (Siegel, 1998). Those who traffick in persons have similar skills. They must be organized with ties to others in the trafficking arena or in the sex trade, and they are willing to take risks for financial gains. Reports from the United Nations' Office on Drugs and Crime (UNODC) (2006) provide evidence of the involvement of organized crime groups in Afghanistan and some of those organized crime units are also involved in human trafficking.

The traditional sources of income for organized crime units are drugs, guns, and sex. According to the Attorney General's Commission on Pornography (1986), most organized crime income is from drug distribution; however, approximately 10 percent of their profits are from the commercial sex industry. As sex trafficking continues to increase, their profits will continue to increase. Organized crime employs predatory tactics such as violence and intimidation and results in economic rewards. It often appeals to individuals desperate for money with few legitimate options for acquiring it. Many families who have women or children victimized through sex trafficking, are also desperate for money. Hence, sex trafficking appeals to many individuals living in Afghanistan.

Finally, corruption is an alarming issue which enables traffickers involved in sex trafficking and/or drug trafficking to transport victims and opiates through local and international borders with ease. With incomes low for many public officials and profits from human trafficking high, it is not unusual for law enforcement and other government officials to become a part of the trafficking network. In other words, the individuals in the best position to end sex trafficking will often facilitate the criminal activity.

Generally speaking, prostitution is the practice of having sexual relations in exchange for money or something else of value. In some countries including the United States, prostitution itself is not a crime, but rather it is the act of soliciting or accepting money that is illegal (Hagan, 1994). Sex trafficking, a concern for many Afghan officials, involves force or coercion to induce a person to perform a sex act. Victims of sex trafficking may be held captive, moved from region to region against their will, and denied the opportunity of escape from the lifestyle of prostitution. In Afghanistan, a country with a male literacy rate of 43 per 100 population and a female literacy rate of 13 per 100 population, the sex trade flourishes with increasing concerns about child sex trafficking.

The Afghan culture is one of male dominance. On average husbands are eight years older than their wives. Husbands are placed in dominant positions of authority over their younger wives (Clarke, 1995). The wives, in turn, move from the dominance of their father's household to the dominance of their husband's household. To extend this culture of male domination and female servitude to the world of commercial sexual exploitation, McCaghy and Hou (1988) suggest that the historical tradition of prostitution in Asia is sanctioned by a patrilineal system that devalues females (adults and children). This devaluing of females remains a part of the Afghan culture. Even today, many women and girls are viewed as property of the male heads of households to exchange or sell if necessary. Afghanistan is a country historically resistant toward any programs even ones of family planning to support females (Mauldin and Ross, 1994). Within that context, the victimization of women through sexual exploitation continues often with families' approval and as a means for securing economic well-being.

Marxist feminist theory is often used to explain the unequal power of men and women in a capitalistic society (Simpson, 1989). In this view, gender inequality is again a function of the exploitation of females by fathers and husbands. An economy of capitalism and the male's desire to achieve success helps to reinforce the inequality. This powerlessness of women increases their likelihood of being a servant, a slave, and a victim.

In summary, one can explain the victimization of women by human traffickers as an outcome of gender bias in a capital system that creates patriarchy and oppresses women (Siegel, 1998). Thus, sex trafficking in Afghanistan can be attributed to many factors including gender inequality, poverty, lack of internal security, and economic opportunities.

Tier Placement

During the twentieth century, there were several hundred cases of human trafficking in Afghanistan; however, there was no single agency or organization responsible for collecting information on human trafficking cases or those offenses related to human trafficking. In response to the lack of consistent reporting, in 2000, President Clinton signed the Trafficking Victims Protection Act (TVPA) which established an Interagency Task Force and the Office to Monitor and Combat Trafficking, the Office, under the Department of State exists to coordinate efforts to reduce human trafficking (McCabe, 2008). The responsibilities of the Office include the classification of countries based upon their progress in addressing human trafficking. To date, over 150 countries are classified based upon information they have provided to the Office with details of each country provided in the Office's *Trafficking in Persons* (TIP) report. Of course, one of the first steps toward ending human trafficking is anti-trafficking legislation.

The classification of countries within the TIP report currently ranks countries as Tier 1, Tier 2, Tier 2 Watch, or Tier 3. Throughout the last five years (2004–2008), Afghanistan has been classified as a Tier 2 country. In 2003, government officials in Afghanistan did not provide the Office to Monitor and Combat Trafficking information on their country and in 2002 Afghanistan was classified as a Tier 3 country. For clarity, Tier 2 countries are countries that do not fully comply with TVPA's minimum standards for addressing human trafficking, but are making significant efforts to do so. Tier 3 countries are those countries that do not comply with TVPA's standards and are not making efforts to comply. Based upon information provided by Afghan officials, the country of Afghanistan is attempting to address human trafficking within their borders. However, their progress has been somewhat stagnant over the last few years with the country officials exerting some efforts to reduce human trafficking, though little in terms of country-wide foci.

The TIP report has identified Afghanistan as a source, transit, and destination country for women and children trafficked for the purposes of sexual exploitation. Afghanistan officials also acknowledge that trafficking of males exists yet suggests that the majority of the sex trafficked victims are female. As a source country, Afghan children are trafficked internally and to the countries of Iran, Pakistan, Saudi Arabia, Omen, and Zimbabwe for both sex and labor. However, many of the reports that have been released are outdated and lacking hard data. This is in part because of the difficulty in obtaining information from those involved in helping to reduce human trafficking and in part due to the very limited geographic access within the country. Afghanistan is a destination country for sexual exploitation for women and girls from China, Iran, and Tajikistan and a transit country for women from Tajikistan who are believed to be trafficked through Afghanistan to Pakistan and Iran. In addition to the economic factors related to the country and the subordinate position of females in the Afghan culture, the physical proximity of Afghanistan to other countries strongly facilitates its utility in the business of sex trafficking. Historically, laws of migration have supported this advantage of adjacent positions or countries. The closer two locations are, the more likely there will exist movement of individuals between them. Specifically, although most people migrate for economic reasons, location is critical and individuals are more likely to move (or be moved) to areas close to their current area. In a country such as Afghanistan, it is predicted that individuals will move or be trafficked to and from bordering countries such as Iran and Pakistan.

Addressing Trafficking

As documented by Afghanistan's consistent classification of Tier 2, the government continues to make some progress in addressing human trafficking although much work is still required. Specifically, in 2004 the government of Italy funded the initial construction of a shelter for child victims of trafficking, and Afghan officials implemented programs to educate teachers on the signs of child trafficking and produced brochures on the risk factors for child trafficking to be distributed to children.

In 2007 the Ministry of Labor and Social Affairs and UNICEF conducted a public awareness campaign to educate the public on dangers of trafficking and resources for assistance. The government of Afghanistan has also recently developed a program to monitor the Afghan-Pakistan and Afghan-Iran borders for victims of trafficking. The government also assisted in supporting approximately 400 child victims of sex trafficking from other source countries by providing them medical and educational services and reuniting them with their families or providing them shelter in juvenile facilities or orphanages. Also in 2007 as a result of international pressures, the government of Afghanistan provided land to the International Organization for Migration (IOM) to construct a shelter for trafficking victims.

Finally, training efforts to standardize and professionalize law enforcement are now under way. However, one must acknowledge that in Afghanistan there is also a very active and lucrative human smuggling network over the Afghan/ Iran border, particularly in the southern regions of Afghanistan. The Iranians forcibly deported over 40,000 of these Afghans in 2008 who were presumable replaced by more Afghans being smuggled across the border with some sort of consent by Iranian authorities. The point is, formal and informal networks are in place and there is essentially no way to successfully interdict at the borders given the tools currently available. Combine that with the fact that most of the Afghans living in Afghanistan see the problems associated with current social conflicts a priority, there is still little in terms of progress to reduce sex trafficking.

The government of Afghanistan has made modest progress in anti-trafficking laws and law enforcement efforts over the past five years, police and prosecutors rely on legislation prohibiting kidnapping to arrest and prosecute traffickers with the assistance of their victims. However, cultural norms and traditions lead to punishment for sexually exploited female victims. Both the Ministry of Interior and the Attorney General's Office have reported that traffickers in Afghanistan have been arrested, prosecuted, and convicted. Unfortunately, few victims have access to legal services in Afghanistan and judicial institutions are weak. In addition, the government reports widespread complicity among border patrols and highway police. Without specific legislation to prohibit human trafficking, Afghanistan's efforts will remain slight in comparison to the prevalence of the problem. Afghanistan must define human trafficking at the legislative level, they must train law enforcement officials on the recognition of human trafficking and they must educate the public on human trafficking. With law enforcement trained and prosecutors educated, Afghanistan may better address the criminal activity of trafficking through and within their borders.

References

Attorney General's Commission on Pornography. (1986). *Final Report.* Washington, DC: US Government Printing Office.

Chaiken, M., and Johnson, B. (1988). *Characteristics of Different Types of Drug-Involved Offenders.* Issues and Practices in Criminal Justice, Washington DC: National Institute of Justice, February.

Clarke, S. (1995). "Advance Report of Final Marriage Statistics, 1989 and 1990." *Monthly Vital Statistics Report,* 43(12, Supplement).

Hagan, F. (1994). *Introduction to Criminology* (3rd ed.). Chicago: Nelson-Hall.

Mauldin, W., and Ross, J. (1994). "Prospects and Programs for Fertility Reduction, 1990–2015." *Studies in Family Planning, 19*:335–353.

McCabe, K. (2008). *The Trafficking of Persons: National and International Responses.* NY: Peter Lang.

McCaghy, C., and Hou, C. (1988). "Cultural Factors and Career Contingencies of Prostitution: The Case of Taiwan." Paper presented at the Society of Criminology Meeting, Chicago, Ill. November.

Sampson, R., and Groves, W. (1989). "Community Structure and Crime: Testing Social Disorganization Theory." *American Journal of Sociology, 94*:774–802.

Siegel, L. (1998). *Criminology. Theories, Patterns, and Typologies* (6th ed.). Belmont, CA: Wadsworth.

Simpson, S. (1989). "Feminist Theory: Crime and Justice." *Criminology, 27*:605–632.

United Nations Office on Drugs and Crime [UNODC]. (2006). *Trafficking in Persons: Global Patterns.* UN: Human Trafficking Unit.

U.S. Department of State. (2008, June). *Trafficking in Persons.* Report. Washington, DC: Office to Monitor and Combat Trafficking in Persons.

VI

WESTERN HEMISPHERE

Kimberly A. McCabe and Sabita Manian

COUNTRIES WITHIN THE WESTERN Hemisphere, in particular countries within the Caribbean are globally recognized as wonderful tourist spots for entertainment, relaxation, and lovely weather. Unfortunately, along with this environment of fun and fantasy is` the underside of exploitation, victimization, and sex trafficking. With the exception of the Bahamas, Haiti, and Barbados, countries within the Western Hemisphere have initiated efforts to address sex trafficking. In fact, in 2008, Colombia was classified as a Tier 1 country. However, the culture of fun and entertainment often associated with this region is one of the most basic underlying conditions that support the criminal activity of sex trafficking. This section provides two chapters—one on the Caribbean and the other on Nicaragua—to provide specific explanations on sex trafficking within the Western Hemisphere.

In the Western Hemisphere, higher class status has historically been reserved for those with lighter skin and for those darker skin individuals, the standards for treatment are lower. Specifically, it is expected that the dark individuals are passionate and always looking for sex (Kempadoo, 2004); thus, they are easy targets for traffickers in search of victims to maintain the highly coveted sex market. Governmental efforts within the countries in the Caribbean are restricted with only a minimal amount of legislative actions to reduce sex trafficking. Law enforcement lacks effectiveness (U.S. Department of State, 2004). As mentioned in other sections of this text, poverty is a factor related to sex trafficking and is also highly visible in the Western Hemisphere. As McCabe (2008) discussed, in areas such as countries in the Western

Hemisphere with military basis, it is not unusual to discover prostitution, pornography, and sex trafficking.

Nicaragua often lacks an effective law enforcement strategy to reduce sex trafficking. Government efforts have only recently begun to address child sex trafficking but not adult trafficking. Immigration services and policies often attempt to address international trafficking; however, without clear distinctions between smuggling and trafficking, sex trafficking victims are often unidentified. In addition, in cases where victims fail to cooperate, efforts end. Cases involving senior government officials are usually not investigated (U.S. Department of State, 2007). Finally, in countries such as Nicaragua with a large proportion of child workers, it is not unusual to discover child victims of sex trafficking. Many individuals, including recruiters, transporters, and parents are involved in the sex trafficking of children (McCabe, 2008). In countries where individuals rely on their children to help support their families, child sex trafficking exists.

Since 2003 to 2007, over 1,200 cases of sex trafficking has been prosecuted in the various countries within this region. Of those cases, approximately 25 percent have resulted in a conviction. In addition, from 2003 to 2007, 31 new or amended legislative actions have been passed to end humans trafficking; however, the incidents within the Western Hemisphere continue to increase. The two chapters in this section discuss sex trafficking in the Western Hemisphere and the commercialization of sex within these specific countries.

References

Kempadoo, K. (2004). *Sexing the Caribbean.* NY: Routledge.

McCabe, K. (2008). *The Trafficking of Persons: National and International Responses.* NY: Peter Lang.

U.S. Department of State (2004, June). *Trafficking in Persons.* Report. Washington, DC: Office to Monitor and Combat Trafficking in Persons.

U.S. Department of State (2007, June). *Trafficking in Persons.* Report. Washington, DC: Office to Monitor and Combat Trafficking in Persons.

12

Sex Traffic and Trafficking in the Caribbean

Brad Bullock

SEX TRAFFICKING IS A COMPLEX GLOBAL phenomenon, best understood on multiple levels and from a variety of approaches. The widespread attention the topic has received fairly recently—from academics, media, governments and law enforcement agencies—is well warranted and based on a recognition that international sex trafficking is becoming more common for some common reasons. And, of course, there are shared features of sex trafficking wherever it appears around the globe: e.g., a connection to prostitution or the illicit sex market.

Most recent studies, though, underscore how sex trafficking and sex work manifest themselves in some very specific ways depending on local context, as evidence from the Caribbean illustrates particularly well. Moreover, while sex trafficking is certainly not new and prostitution is often called "the oldest profession," their global reinvention today is thoroughly new—both postindustrial and postmodern.

This chapter focuses on the Caribbean sex trade, which cannot be viewed properly without some historical perspective and a full discussion of citizenship, class, race, and gender. From this wider vantage the Caribbean, by comparison to other regions, is both similar and quite distinct. The most important distinction is that the Caribbean problem is not so much sex trafficking but rather *sex traffic*, encouraged by strategies to increase revenues from tourism. This point is crucial, especially if the goal is curtailing abusive practices. We'll focus on The Dominican Republic since it enjoys a dubious distinction as the Caribbean's "sex capital" and because it well represents the complicated (and sometimes contradictory) characteristics of the Caribbean sex trade.

The primary purpose here is not just to offer an overview of issues, but also a framework for sorting "the facts" one might easily gather in an afternoon surfing the web. Unfortunately, sex trafficking and sex work are usually presented from only one or two angles (e.g., merely a function of poverty or a modern form of slavery where female victims are duped, forced, or coerced into prostitution). Without question, poverty does fuel the global sex trade, its victims are overwhelmingly women, and they are tricked or forced into it against their will. Failing to go beyond these observations, however, misses more subtle ways that women and the people in their lives may suffer. Such a limited view does not adequately address causes that spur the modern sex trade, nor give a complete picture of it (including female agency and complicity); nor does it, finally, suffice for deciding how best to address the many problems tied to it.

We must, for starters, understand how the Caribbean fits into a fully globalized, international economy shaped by colonial history and the region's proximity to the United States of America. In absolute numbers, Caribbean women (e.g., from the DR and neighboring Haiti) constitute a small share of international sex trafficking victims, yet they are wildly overrepresented (relative to the size of their populations) in sex trafficking routes to EU countries. This relative demand is intimately linked to rising sex traffic *into* the Caribbean, from sex tourists who feed sexual stereotypes and create the demand. Sex tourists largely shape Caribbean sex trade practices and responses to them (e.g., any criminal implications) and trade on their higher status relative to those providing sex. Ultimately, all aspects of the sex trade—trafficking, sex tourism, prostitution, and "voluntary" sex work—are powered by such global inequalities. These inequalities, in turn, are fueled by ongoing economic and political disruptions. In this sense, the existing sex trade is an international security issue tied to other such issues: for example, public health as it concerns HIV/AIDS transmission.

Sex trafficking and much of the sex trade is hidden and difficult to document, so figures vary widely. The DR, along with Haiti and Jamaica, are notable source countries, but most of the women trafficked to the North or other places know generally what they're getting into (in contrast to stories of being duped or sold, which is more true of Asia; see Kara, 2009). One reasonable estimate is that at any given time about 50,000 Dominican women are engaging in sex work outside the DR, with perhaps a third operating outside the Caribbean (Kempadoo, 2004; USDS). Most Dominicans migrate for sex work *within* the Caribbean— working in brothels, hotels, and bars in places like Haiti, Curacao, Antigua, and Surinam—or within the DR, typically from rural areas to tourist sites. Haitians and Jamaicans also migrate into the DR for sex work. Gregory (2007) conservatively estimates that annually "tens of thousands" of sex tourists visit the DR, while estimates for the region run into the hundreds of thousands.

Caribbean Context

The Caribbean is actively constructed as a "hypersexual," tropical paradise, making sex traffic and trafficking more likely. Exotic black and brown bodies, racialized "others" in this construction, engage in casual sex because it's in their nature, excessive sex for them is "normal" and, after all, the Caribbean is a place where "anything goes." Excellent work led by Kempadoo (e.g., 2004; 1999) relates ways, within this construct, that gender and race interact to affect perception and practice. She emphasizes that what is simultaneously sold and perpetuated is "hetero-patriarchy," a system where dominant, straight (white) males rule. Whether from a brothel in Germany or a tourist hotel in the DR, the fantasy is that deferent Caribbean women prefer aggressive men who dominate them. Ironically, local Caribbean men and the institutions they control help preserve this view of women and gender relations for the foreigners who exploit them, sometimes violently. Research suggests that many men (mostly from Europe and North America) seek sex from such women in response to "liberated" women from their own countries who embody higher expectations and more demands (e.g., Brennan, 2004).

Northern citizenship, and the class inequality it represents, also lends an inherent advantage in sexual transactions over those in the South (any Caribbean country); this is particularly so for whites. Brennan (2004) raises this important question: why should so many European men travel all the way to the Caribbean for sex when such women are readily available in Europe? Her answer: the Caribbean represents a "sexscape" where sex is cheap, unlimited male access to it goes unchallenged, and there's the thrill of class inversion—a working-class male reinvents himself abroad as a player with means, gaining the power or respect this implies.

Not all sex trafficking is forced or hidden, and not all sex work is prostitution in the conventional, Western sense (sex acts for money) by women trapped into the practice. Historically, the Caribbean combines colonial and local, cultural traditions, producing a wide variety of intimate arrangements, sexual and otherwise. Colonial plantation systems created social disruptions among workers' families (through sale, death, or migration for work) and imposed the social value of lighter skin. High levels of migration, both within the Caribbean and to the North, are a long-standing fact. This helped solidify matrifocal, single female headed households and led to survival strategies that encourage traditions of multipartnering (with men), multiple means of support (e.g., female family members), and migrating for work. Especially for women, who lacked formal employment options, negotiating goods and services informally (including sex) has always been essential. Seeking temporary sex work abroad is not surprising, and Brennan sees the current sex trade not

just as an extension of slavery but of long-established customs in the entertainment or hospitality industries (2004). Thus, generally, South serves North,
women serve men, and dark serves white.

The DR illustrates how skin color and race influence the sex trade locally
and across borders. At sex tourism sites (e.g., Sosua and Boca Chica), lighter-
skinned Dominicans are favored over usually darker, poorer Haitians. Haitians are likely forced to work the streets or local bars rather than more lucrative tourist sites and are more likely hassled by authorities; Dominican racial
prejudice plays a large role in this. Government-approved agents actively recruit Dominican women using temporary sex work contracts for a legalized
brothel in Curacao, whereas darker Haitians are deemed unacceptable. Kempadoo reports that, since the 1960s, all of the workers in Curacao's "Campo
Allegre" are either from the DR or Colombia. Authorities in Curacao, including church authorities, ultimately rationalized legalized sex camps filled with
foreign workers as a means of protecting local women (Kempadoo, 2004).

U.S. imperialism of the early twentieth century helped lay groundwork for
Caribbean sex camps and the identification of light-skinned Dominicans as
desirable. Military occupation of the DR and Curacao around WWI established a "need" to service the foreign visitors (much as they service sex tourists
today). The military likewise played an important role in securing U.S. control
over local commodities, like the Dominican sugar industry. Then, and later—
under the control of the U.S.-backed dictator Trujillo—common sugar workers continued to lead harsh lives of limited opportunities, making migration
and black market activities attractive (Gregory, 2007). Later, when sugar
crashed under the weight of global competition, there were few immediate
options for the DR beyond tourism, and attaching "sex" to the foreign vaca-
tion has admittedly given the DR a niche in the now saturated Caribbean
tourist industry. In some countries tourism accounts for up to 70 percent of
GNP, and the tourist sector is estimated to account for ¼ of all formal employment in the DR (Kempadoo, 2004).

Caribbean concepts of sexual labor are broad, as are expected rewards
from a diverse set of practices. Sex work is usually just one part of survival
strategies—practiced temporarily while engaging in other economic activities—and women often have some control over sex practices. Sex work is not
just driven by poverty, but is commonly pursued by women and men as a
strategy for advancement (Kempadoo, 2004; Brennan, 2004). Most Dominican women Kempadoo encountered in Curacao were there either to pay off
debts or put away some money for starting legitimate businesses back home.
Unlike brothel-style prostitution (sex exchanged for cash from strangers), the
primary goal for those servicing sex tourists is establishing several ongoing
relationships; rewards may be indirectly monetary and based on a developing

familiarity or the client's length of stay. Money may be exchanged along the way, or wired from abroad over an extended period, but other immediate rewards include gifts of clothes, dinners out, activities in expensive resorts, or accessories for children and the household. Locals refer euphemistically to "working with tourists" in roles as "hostesses" or "guides;" established relationships abroad are those with "boyfriends." Kempadoo cites a study where fewer than 5 percent of female sex workers surveyed in the DR and Jamaica identified their sexual encounters as purely physical or "just about sex," preferring to speak of special friendships or romances (2004: 128). Brennan reveals how they practice "performing romance," speak earnestly about caring for foreign "boyfriends," and provide men with nonsexual intimacy.

Research by Gregory (2007) and Padilla (2007) concerning male sex workers in the DR (usually called "sanky-pankies") reveal similar findings: these men generally don't identify themselves as sex workers and seek continuing relationships, with the interesting difference that they frequently serve both male and female tourists. The big prize, especially for women, is the security of marriage to a wealthy foreigner, or a relationship resulting in a visa to leave the island for an idealized, better life in the North. In Brennan's experiences, gaining a green card is something of a national pastime in the DR, where nearly every sex worker she met was a single mother (2004).

Work by LaFont (2002) and others draws a distinction between sex tourism developed to serve men and "romance tourism" catering more to women. Female tourists find real or perceived romances a compelling fantasy for relationships that usually include sexual transactions but not direct payments for sex. Successful "sankies" learn "the performance of love" and are adept at providing an intimacy "girlfriends" respond to with gifts, clothing, or money for nonsexual activities. In these exchanges, female tourists also count on superior status, where white trumps black and Northern citizenship trumps all. Female sex tourism turns local gender hierarchy on its head, since women hold power over local men used to being in control. Here's one reason sankies deny their identity as sex workers and reset themselves as "players" with strings of girlfriends (Padilla, 2007). The DR is a major tourist destination for gay men, and sanky-pankies do provide homoerotic sex for them, but the majority of sankies are not gay and many struggle to maintain relationships with wives or local girlfriends even while engaging in these practices. In this case, they typically portray themselves as entrepreneurs and hustlers getting the better of gay tourists.

Whether a sex worker is female or male, families and friends usually know about their activities, and several scholars speak about the uneasy silence families keep (e.g., Brennan, 2004; Padilla, 2007). Frequently, female family members even facilitate sex work with tourists by babysitting, providing fashion advice, or setting up meetings with potential clients. In contrast to a sex trade in Europe and Asia controlled almost exclusively by men, the DR features "businesses" or arrangements in the hands of women. Yet in the Caribbean sex industry, men still control bars, hotels, and other sites where sex tourism typically transpires and men reap most of the benefits as business owners, taxi drivers, police officers and other government officials who expect a cut. Brennan similarly makes this point: whereas male sex tourists typically get what they seek, female sex workers usually don't (Dominican women complain that local men are unreliable, but support from foreign men is similarly unreliable).

Global Context

In today's truly global economy, powerful countries in the postindustrial North continue to look South for cheap sources of labor and commodities. Trends like outsourcing, development of Free Trade Zones (FTZs), and technological innovations like the internet have influenced the Caribbean sex trade in several ways.

The latest chapter of development history finds typical Caribbean economies strapped by lingering foreign debt (roundly encouraged by Northern policy makers) and the need to make up for revenue shortfalls in fiercely competitive commodity markets, especially for traditional agricultural exports. Lately, the same agencies and policy experts have demanded extensive cuts in government spending (known as "structural adjustment programs" or SAPs) as a condition for lending additional funds. These imposed restructurings curtailed social spending on the working poor even as unemployment in traditional export industries hit historic levels.

One "solution" was FTZs, where Northern corporations (lured by cheap labor and tax incentives) outsource production of clothing, electronics, or other goods to places like the DR. This created a shift in employment, since Northern companies predominantly hired female workers and male labor declined along with export production. The other viable option for expanding revenues was tourism, and foreign investors poured billions into it. What had been a marginal industry in the DR before the 1980s quickly became its largest single source of revenue, eclipsing sugar exports. As with corporations operating in FTZs, the tourist industry is mostly foreign owned and controlled ("all-inclusive" resorts, a prime example) and women outnumber men as employees. It would seem that such trends provide a boon for women, but in reality they have helped encourage sex trafficking and sex work for the simple reason that the latter is often deemed the better option.

Dominican women laboring in FTZs and tourist resorts (e.g., maids, waitresses) routinely face sexual exploitation, harassment, and humiliation from employers and patrons alike. Pay for the long hours—sometimes in difficult conditions—is often insufficient to meet a family's basic needs. Doing sex work with tourists, women earn in a night or weekend what it would take a week or more to earn formally employed, and they have more control over hours and working conditions. Also, they don't have to be trafficked illegally abroad, far away from their families.

The advent of the internet is intertwined with the growth of Caribbean sex trafficking and sex traffic. Numerous official and unofficial sites stoke the Caribbean "fantasy industry," feeding the hypersexual construction of the place and its people. Other technological innovations (fax machines, cell phones, digital money transfers) are likewise indispensable to the sex trade. Yet the current commodification of sex and sex work is thoroughly postmodern, not just because of new technologies but because of the internationalization of tourists who view sex with locals as just another form of consumption.

Rights and Security

Sex trafficking usually brings to mind the violation of the rights and freedoms of women and children sold or smuggled illegally and forced into prostitution, along with other international security threats like drug trafficking, organized crime, refugee conflicts, and even terrorism. While these remain serious threats worldwide, they don't characterize the Caribbean.

Based on protocols established by the 2000 Trafficking Victim and Protection Act, the DR is repeatedly cited for incidents of *sex trafficking and prostitution, children exploited for commercial sex,* and *child sex tourism* in annual Trafficking in Persons (TIP) reports authored by the U.S. State Department (USDS). Stories featuring the complicity of major business owners and corrupt government officials who go unprosecuted or unpunished are routine.

After beginning the decade on the Tier 2 list, the DR was downgraded to Tier 3 in 2003, and did enough publicly to restore a Tier 2 ranking in 2004; since then, it mostly occupies the Tier 2 Watch list. A significant change of categorization in 2003—from trafficking "source" to a "source, transit, and destination" country—negatively affects the DR's ranking, since it's mainly faulted in recent TIP reports for "not doing enough" on several fronts.

Begun with good intentions, the USDS tier rankings have become thoroughly politicized and surprisingly arbitrary (at best, representing an incomplete picture of sex trafficking and only a rudimentary typology for trafficking offenses). Caribbean governments must pay attention to these rankings since, directly or indirectly, they can affect eligibility for loans or other programs.

But using them to assess progress in sex trafficking or to determine policy is fraught with numerous difficulties.

There is no doubt that the DR has serious problems with sex trafficking and human smuggling that sometimes involves young children, nor is there doubt that corrupt officials participate in the sex trade. Yet women (much less children), duped and smuggled against their will, is not the typical Caribbean case and partially explains why Caribbean scholars generally give the TIP rankings little credence.

Reports conflate sex trafficking with trafficking for other purposes and define "child" by the culturally-debatable age of 18. Actual statistics are rare and unstandardized; they vary widely from year to year, partly since numbers come inconsistently from various NGOs. Unsubstantiated or undefined qualifiers abound (*"some* are trafficked," *"many* children are victimized"). There are also numerous conflicts of interest: e.g., it's in the interest of the United States to show it's serious about holding traffickers accountable, and many NGOs doing vital work for which they must raise money are more likely to find and count "victims" (women exercising "choice" in "sex work" is not a compelling moral tale). Finally, the DR's officials must show interest in "progress" toward curtailing trafficking in the same sex trade that provides a substantial portion of domestic revenue and foreign currency (if also the livelihoods of corrupt agents).

Since most of those migrating for sex work are of legal age and exercise some choice (albeit within a complicated calculus of other limited choices), the main security issue remains smuggling and illegal documents for access to sex markets, but this is more an issue within the region, where illegal crossings are commonplace. Ironically, international debt and subsequent SAPs imposed on countries like the DR have done two things: made remittances from Dominican nationals abroad (including sex workers) more important to the government in the face of limited spending, and redirected resources that could have gone toward better enforcement of trafficking violations.

The underlying issue is one of worker's rights, increasingly a women's issue in both the formal and informal economies. Aradau (2007) suggests that presenting sex work as forced prostitution and victimization by illegal, international syndicates serves the agendas of certain international agencies, rights groups, and governments demonstrating "action" against security threats. She calls this "politics masked as security," since underlying local and global inequities that encourage the continued exploitation of sex workers remain unaddressed. The alternative view promotes a struggle to recognize sex workers as workers (Augustin, 2002; Kempadoo and Doezema, 1998).

Certainly the spread of AIDS is a legitimate international security issue. Given the sheer volume of sex traffic, combined with persistent want and status inequalities between buyers and sellers of sex, it's unsurprising that the Caribbean HIV infection rate is second worldwide, behind Africa (and over 40 times that for Latin America). Rates are highest among frequent migrants, and Padilla (2007) contends that sanky-pankies' bisexual activities are an underexplored vector for HIV transmission.

Conclusion

Features of the global economy, Northern economic policies, and even Northern social movements for gay or women's rights, have combined with aspects of the Caribbean culture to create conditions ripe for a booming sex trade. Kempadoo (2004:85) states: ". . . despite national and international efforts to curtail, limit, and control women's sexual-economic activities, sex work has a long history and is deeply embedded in social relations. It is thus likely to continue [as] an integral part of the Caribbean landscape into the future." Ultimately, persistent global inequalities drive all aspects of the sex trade, and policies aimed at its unsavory abuses must concentrate on ameliorating these inequalities. In a real sense, sex workers serving tourists still represents the North exploiting cheap labor, and sex tourism a type of outsourcing. Dependency on tourism and the lack of other employment opportunities for women and men make sex traffic and sex trafficking only more likely.

References

Aradau, C. (2007). *Rethinking Trafficking in the Caribbean.* NY: Macmillan.

Augustin, L. (2002). *Sex at the Margins.* NY: Zed Books.

Brennan, D. (2004). *What's Love Got to Do with It?* Durham: Duke University Press.

Gregory, S. (2007). *The Devil Behind the Mirror.* Los Angeles: University of California Press.

Kara, S. (2009). *Sex Trafficking.* NY: Columbia University Press.

Kempadoo, K. (1999). *Sun, Sex, and Gold.* NY: Rowman & Littlefield.

Kempadoo, K. (2004). *Sexing the Caribbean.* NY: Routledge.

Kempadoo, K., and Doezema, J. (eds.). (1998). *Global Sex Workers.* NY: Routledge.

LaFont, S. (2002). *Constructing Sexualities.* NY: Prentice Hall.

Padilla, M. (2007). *Caribbean Pleasure Industry.* IL: University of Chicago Press.

13

Child Commercial Sexual Exploitation in Nicaragua: A Critical Globalization Perspective

Mirna Carranza and Henry Parada

THE INCORPORATION OF COMMERCIAL sexual exploitation of children (CSEC), including child sex tourism (CST), into the economies of tourist destination countries is a little understood phenomenon (Kempadoo, 2004). One barrier faced by those attempting to understand the problem of CSEC is a dearth of local information about its nature and incidence, in spite of evidence of its existence. Moreover, although a growing body of literature sheds light on structural inequalities at the heart of the sex trade industry globally, including global economic disparities, the prevalence of violence against women and children, gender inequality, heterosexism, and racism (Ellsberg, 2005; Estes and Weiner, 2003; Torres-Saillant, 2006; Vos, 1999), little is known about how local realities intersect with structural, global issues to shape the nature of CSEC in specific countries.

According to the UN's International Labour Organization (ILO, 2003), roughly 1.8 million children worldwide are exploited in the multibillion dollar commercial sex industry, which includes child sex tourism (Gregory, 2007; ILO, 2003). Global responses from governments, law enforcement, and NGOs have increased prosecution of CST charges, but CST is still a major problem in many regions of the world, including Nicaragua ("Trafficking," 2005).

Though globalization research has generated much evidence of the deleterious impact of economic and trade liberalization on the global South, advocates of a *critical globalization* perspective would have us ask to what extent such research has simultaneously advanced global social activism (Chun, 2004; Mensah, Prempeh, and Adjibolosoo, 2004). Critical globalization scholars challenge researchers to do research that (a) is informed by the links between global processes and local realities and (b) engages in critical analysis of global forces so that social justice and human rights are promoted (Yashar, 2005).

Yashar (2005) argued that because the impact of globalization is not homogenous, it is best explored in relation to national and local communities (in this case, Nicaragua). The simple idea that globalization is occurring is not enough to explain many local dynamics, because "questions of place and scale [of the effect of globalization] are not self evident" (Kirsch, 2006, p. 6). Applying a critical globalization perspective to the problem of child sexual exploitation allows for the exploration of why and how local actors respond to external forces of global capitalism and neoliberalism (Yashar, 2005). In the case of Nicaragua, global inequalities created by the forces of globalization and neoliberalism have resulted in increased sex tourism in Central America generally (Altman, 2001; Kempadoo, 2004).

The political economy of sexuality, which situates CSEC and sex tourism within the socioeconomic and political contexts that create the conditions for such exploitation, is useful for explaining the links between sex tourism and globalization (Altman, 2001; Monzini, 2005). The economy of sexuality is closely related to the labor roles assigned to countries in Central America within the global economy—namely tourism—and to power relations that subordinate women, children, and ethnoracial minorities (Bambas, Casas, Drayton, and Valdez, 2000; Sabbagh, 2004; Steinberg, 2005).

The dynamics involved in CSEC within this economic strategy are not well understood. Feminist postdevelopment and poststructural thought are useful for understanding the factors influencing the social and political legitimization of CSEC. In general, when studying the exploitation of people in southern countries, postdevelopment scholars contend that factors such as gender inequity, colonial relations, and economic systems need to be examined (Brysk, 2005; Fischlin and Nandorfy, 2007; Kirsch, 2006; Saunders, 2002; Yashar, 2005).

Central American Context

Over the last several years, government officials in Central America, in collaboration with international NGOs and local civil society organizations, have engaged in the development of legislation and programs to improve the protection of children and reduce interfamilial violence within the poorest communities in their countries. Many of these policies and programs are also closely linked to health promotion issues, especially the reduction of HIV/AIDS. However, few results have been achieved to date. There has been limited implementation of policies in a manner that can produce significant improvement for children and women.

Government officials in Central America face many challenges regarding the implementation and evaluation of new policies and programs that would reduce and eradicate trafficking in children and women and protect them from extreme forms of labor exploitation and sexual exploitation. These governments have expressed their commitment to ensuring the protection of children and women by signing and ratifying international conventions. They have also implemented a series of legal framework reforms, including laws for the protection of children, laws against intrafamilial violence, and laws against the trafficking of people for labor and sexual exploitation. But levels of poverty in Nicaragua (where half the population lives in extreme poverty on $1 a day), natural disasters (in 1998, Hurricane Mitch destroyed 40 percent of the country's agriculture and infrastructure), and issues of governance and migration have affected the successful implementation of these legal frameworks to protect children and women.

Trafficking in Central America appears to involve high numbers of children for sexual and labor exploitation. The sex trade is the principal area of exploitation of underage girls, particularly in areas where the tourism industry is developing, such as the Pacific areas of Nicaragua. The demand for sexual services is concentrated in areas known as *zones of tolerance*, which include tourist areas and ports along the costal areas of Nicaragua (OAS, 2003).

An area of concern that is evident in Nicaragua, as in other countries in Central America and the Caribbean, is that domestic trafficking (from rural to tourist areas of the country) involves increasing numbers of children. Factors contributing to the sexual exploitation of children and women include gender inequality, poverty, demand for sexual services, misuse of the Internet, family breakdown, and the lure of easy money, but the most important factor is a high level of poverty in the country.

The ILO (2003) subregional report found that one form of labor exploitation particularly affecting girls was child domestic labor. Although in most Latin American societies, children perform activities around the house, recent studies have indicated that children employed in households other than their own as domestic servants are at risk in several ways. These children are removed from their own families and have no protection from employers who may abuse them sexually, physically, or emotionally. In addition, they work long hours, engage in onerous tasks, and are fed poorly.

Research in Latin American countries found that although more young boys ages 7 to 17 work outside the home, the participation of young girls, particularly those under the age of 12, is suspected to be widely underreported, because girls often work in their own or other families' homes and are not reported or regarded as workers. The relationship between education and child labor is an important component. Failure in school, repetition of grades, falling behind, low academic achievement, and dropping out of school characterize working children, especially the poorest ones (Inter-American, 2005).

Central American countries face several challenges in the implementation of laws to protect women and children. The following challenges have been identified in Central America:

1. There is a lack of databases for information that would provide understanding of child protection needs.
2. Statistics do not accurately quantify the magnitude of the trafficking in children and women.
3. Dissemination of information to law enforcement practitioners, educators, researchers, and the community is not done systematically.
4. Government authorities have failed to use the data developed by NGOs.
5. The trafficking of women and children for commercial sexual exploitation has not been considered a high priority on the national agendas. (OAS, 2003)

We believe the research we are proposing would be of value to agencies and organizations that work with women and children.

Nicaragua

Gender and poverty are at the forefront of CSEC in Nicaragua. According to UNICEF (2003), Nicaragua's most pressing challenge is to overcome poverty and inequality, which disproportionately affect women and children. Nicaragua is the third poorest country in the Americas, with an income distribution that is one of the most unequal in the world (UNICEF, 2003). More than 50 percent of the total population (that is, approximately 2.9 million individuals) are under 19 years of age, and lack of family and state resources prevent approximately 4 out of 10 children and adolescents from attending school (*Review of Child Labour*, 2006). Adolescent births account for 1 in 4 births nationally, and approximately 85 percent of all Nicaraguan mothers are single mothers (*Review of Child Labour*, 2006; UNICEF, 2003). Poor, single mothers may be forced to agree to CSEC out of necessity, making it a classed and gendered occupation on the margins of Nicaraguan society (Bruckert and Parent, 2006).

The fact that girls and female youth are the primary victims of CSEC is normalized by the general population through perceptions of CSEC as a normal woman's role, helping the family, or the belief that the victims have a high sexual libido (Help Resources, 2005; Nokomis Foundation, 2002). These popular beliefs tend to blame victims of CSEC without considering the context in which the exploitation takes place or the fact that exposure to intrafamilial violence, a primary cause of divorce and separation in Nicaragua, may distort perceptions among youth and children who see CSEC as a continuation of what they consider to be normal family dynamics (*Review of Child Labour*, 2006). Such misconceptions cast CSEC as a choice that often results from a lack of parental guidance. Consequently, a primary focus of research in this area should be clarifying how gender, oppression, and poverty intersect to sustain CSEC.

Added to the socioeconomic conditions that contribute to CSEC are the apathy and inefficiency of the judicial system, which arguably plays a large role in the continuation of child prostitution. Nicaragua has developed many initiatives to reduce CSEC; however, these are not systematized and, historically, have been largely ineffective (Rojas, 2007; Sevilla, 2007). The Nicaraguan government has responded to pressure from international figures and foundations (e.g., the Ricky Martin Foundation) and international feminist grass roots movements (e.g., the Miriam Association), but the eradication of CSEC is not part of the government's political agenda. Speculation among NGOs and concerned Nicaraguan citizens is that the government receives such a lucrative income from the tourist sector participating in CSEC that they are unwilling to fully support its eradication. The fact that prostitution is legal for those 14 years and over would seem to support this claim (A. I. Torres, personal communication, April 12, 2007). The promotion of prostitution for those 14 years of age and older is also legal; however, CSEC (i.e., involving juveniles under 14 years of age) is illegal. In 2004, the government approved Article 203 of the Penal Code, which criminalized CSEC and provided for 3 to 5 years of jail time; in 2006, Article 182 was approved, increasing the penalty for those convicted of CSEC to 7 to 10 years' imprisonment (Moreno, 2008). Despite these legal provisions, prosecution of CSEC cases is rare (Sanchez, 2007).

In 2006, under mounting international pressure, the Nicaraguan government launched a massive capacity-building effort to educate police officers and judges about the nature of CSEC and to encourage the full enforcement of the law in CSEC cases. In the same year, they launched a national educational campaign against CSEC, funded by the Ricky Martin Foundation. A 24-hour anti-trafficking hotline was developed to provide services for victims of trafficking and exploitation. In two months the hotline received 690 calls related to CSEC (A. I. Torres, personal communication, April 12, 2007). Another initiative, led by concerned members of Nicaraguan civil society partnered with local NGOs, launched national campaigns to raise awareness among vulnerable populations about potential lures into CSEC, pressure government officials to enforce the law on perpetrators, and challenge Nicaragua's tolerance for CSEC (Barrantes, 2007).

The province of Esteli has taken the lead on several initiatives to stem CSEC. Among these are campaigns by Ixchen (an NGO) to enhance the community's awareness about CSEC, and public protests organized by the Miriam Association (Mujeres, 2007). Efforts throughout Nicaragua suffer from poor coordination, communication, and information about CSEC. Government officials, who are limited in their roles, are appealing to local NGOs and international governments for support in the protection of children exploited through CSEC, but local NGOs generally fail to effectively engage and empower vulnerable communities (Moreno, 2008).

In this context, it can be argued that the global dynamics of tourism have resulted in a sex industry that is needed by families who have few other opportunities to survive and escape from poverty, both locally and on a national scale (Brennan, 2004; Pruitt and LaFont, 1995). In some areas of Nicaragua, the sex trade is the only work available, and in some cases it has become a labor role through which citizens are able to recognize themselves as having a productive value (*Reporte de la Explotación*, 2005). The sex trade is not only an activity of the participants, but it becomes, in part, how the participants make sense of their identity and significance to their family and community (Brennan, 2004).

O'Connell (2005) used a poststructural frame to argue that we need to recognize children as unique agents in order to grasp the complexity of the links between the sex trade and risk factors such as poverty, neglect, abuse, homophobia, and racism. This perspective will allow us to explore the nature, causes, and meaning of diversity in the children's sexual oppression.

To deal with the social category of *child* as a monolithic, homogenous group may result in overlooking the realities of many of these children's lived experiences in different countries and societies. Because the engagement of global forces, the relations of people transnationally, and the subject location of citizens is not decided *a priori*, both the local assumptions shaping the sex trade and the global forces that make it possible are open to analysis. It is imperative that an approach to the study of CSEC be taken that allows for the examination of the forces of global relations, empirically at the local level, in order to better understand the actors involved and the power relationships that are at play (Radcliffe, 2001).

As we have argued, CSEC and CST are issues that must be understood as products of both local and global factors. CSEC is part of a global phenomenon in which Canadians are implicated and for which Canada must accept social responsibility. In fact, Canadians are considered to be the third largest consumers of sex tourism (Brennan, 2004; Gregory, 2007). Canada has taken steps toward eradicating CSEC, such as Criminal Code provisions allowing for the arrest and prosecution of Canadians in Canada for CST-related offenses committed in foreign countries (Foreign Affairs, 2007). Reports and accounts in the international literature help to shape our understanding of the context within which CSEC is occurring, but it is also crucial that data collection be done on site, so that we can understand what is actually happening on the ground. We do not know enough about the individual children involved in CSEC in Nicaragua (e.g., their age, background, sex, health status, education level, and history of abuse and neglect) to understand why foreign tourists consider such children legitimate sexual objects. A necessary first step in understanding such dynamics is the assessment of the incidence of CSEC and gaining a better picture of the children involved (Flisher, 2005; Jejeebhoy and Bott, 2005).

Factors affecting the incidence of CSEC should be carefully considered within the local realities of each country. The dynamics of child exploitation in Nicaragua is qualitatively different from that in other countries (See Table 1). Within this context, the demand and the kind of demand that emerges is important. For example, anecdotal evidence suggests that Nicaraguan boys are taken to Costa Rica and girls are taken to El Salvador and the tourism areas of Nicaragua (*Informe*, 2007).

However, little is known about the characteristics of the perpetrator, that is, the man who seeks out children for sexual pleasure and feelings of power. In addition, the fact that Nicaragua was involved in a cruel and lengthy war, as well as issues of race and ethnicity (among others), need to be included in the analysis of factors impacting CSEC.

Conclusions

Concerned members of Nicaraguan civil society and feminist grassroots organizations are pressuring the Nicaraguan government to fully enforce Articles 203 and 182 of the penal code. NGOs are working at full capacity to develop the necessary protocols and practices to effectively deal with CSEC. However, CSEC cannot be eradicated without the support of the international community (e.g., holding citizens of all countries fully accountable for crimes committed against children in foreign lands, providing financial resources to grassroots movements and local NGOs in developing countries) and the support of the Nicaraguan government to fully enforce the existing laws and to allocate the necessary resources (e.g., human resources and infrastructures). Otherwise the sexual commodification of the bodies of vulnerable children will continue to prevail.

TABLE 13.1
Factors Impacting CSEC in Nicaragua

Kinds of factors	Examples
Socioeconomic	Extreme poverty Unemployment Lack of employment stability Globalization Labor migration
Sociocultural	Patriarchy Gender inequalities Power relationships between employer and employee Legacy of colonialism High tolerance for and lack of understanding of CSEC by the general population Religion: High emphasis on obedience and submission Culture of violence Illiteracy Proliferation of nightclubs Drug & alcohol misuse Taboos & lack of knowledge about sexuality
Family	Domestic violence *Hacinamiento* (Several families living in a small space) High level of family disintegration due to divorce and migration
Legal	Weak legal system Lack of application of the penal codes Corruption within the system

Source: Adapted from *Reporte de la Explotación Sexual, Comercial de la Niñez en Nicaragua,* 2005, Managua, Nicaragua

There is a need for research that addresses the global inequalities created by the forces of neoliberalism and globalization in increasing sex tourism across the globe. The utilization of a critical globalization perspective that would advance global social activism is also essential (Chun, 2004; Mensah et al., 2004).

References

Altman, D. (2001). *Global sex.* Chicago: University of Chicago Press.

Bambas, A., Casas, J. A., Drayton, H. A., and Valdez, A. (2000). *Health and human development in the new global economy.* Washington, DC: World Health Organization.

Barrantes, D. (2007). *Campaña para llamar a la sociedad a combatir explotación sexual infantil.* Managua, Nicaragua.

Brennan, D. (2004). *What's love got to do with it? Transnational desires and sex tourism in the Dominican Republic*. Durham, NC: Duke University Press.

Bruckert, C., and Parent, C. (2006). The in-call sex industry: Classed and gendered labour on the margins. In G. Balfour and E. Comack (Eds.), *Criminalizing women: Gender and (in)justice in neo-liberal times* (pp. 95–112). Halifax, NS, Canada: Fernwood.

Brysk, A. (2005). *Human rights and private wrongs: Constructing global civil society*. New York: Routledge.

Child prostitution: The commercial sexual exploitation of children: Republic of Nicaragua. <http://gvnet.com/childprostitution/Nicaragua.htm> (6 Sept. 2008).

Chun, A. J. U. L. (2004). *Globalization: Critical issues*. New York: Berghahn Books.

Ellsberg, M. (2005). Sexual violence against women and girls: Recent findings from Latin America and the Caribbean. In S. J. Jejeebhoy, I. H. Shah, and S. Thapa (Eds.), *Sex without consent: Young people in developing countries* (pp. 49–58). New York: Zed Books.

Estes, R., and Weiner, N. (2003). La explotación sexual comercial de los niños en Estados Unidos. In R. Estes and E. Azaola (Eds.), *La infancia como mercancía sexual: México, Canadá, Estados Unidos* (pp. 44–90). Mexico City, Mexico: Siglo Veintiuno.

Fischlin, D., and Nandorfy, M. (2007). *The concise guide to global human rights*. Montreal, QC, Canada: Black Rose Books.

Flisher, A. (2005). Non-consensual experiences: Policy implications. In S. J. Jejeebhoy, I. H. Shah, and S. Thapa (Eds.), *Sex without consent: Young people in developing countries* (pp. 269–284). New York: Zed Books.

Foreign Affairs and International Trade Canada. (2007). *Sexual exploitation of children*. <http://www.dfait-maeci.gc.ca/foreign_policy/> (6 Sept. 2008).

Gregory, S. (2007). *The devil behind the mirror: Globalization and politics in the Dominican Republic*. Berkeley: University of California Press.

Gulbenkian, F. C. (2005, March). *Tráfico de seres humanos y migraciones: Un análisis desde la perspectiva de los derechos humanos*. Paper presented at the conference on Tráfico de Seres Humanos y Migraciones, Lisbon, Portugal.

Help Resources. (2005). *A situational analysis of child sexual abuse & commercial sexual exploitation in Papua New Guinea*. Unpublished report.

Informe sobre la trata de personas. (2007). Managua, Nicaragua: Comunidades eclesiásticas de base.

Inter-American Development Bank Education Unit. (2005). *Expanding the knowledge capital of Latin America and the Caribbean: An IDB Strategy for education and training*. Sustainable Development Department.

International Labour Organization. (2003). *Explotación sexual comercial de personas menores de edad en la Republica Dominicana*. Panama City, Panama: Author.

Jejeebhoy, S., and Bott, S. (2005). Non-consensual experiences of young people in developing countries: An overview. In S. J. Jejeebhoy, I. H. Shah, and S. Thapa (Eds.), *Sex without consent: Young people in developing countries* (pp. 3–46). New York: Zed Books.

Kempadoo, K. (2004). *Sexing the Caribbean: Gender, race and sexual labor*. New York: Routledge.

Kirsch, M. (2006). Inclusion and exclusion in the global arena. In M. Kirsch (Ed.), *Inclusion and exclusion in the global arena* (pp. 1–27). New York: Routledge.

Kuo, L. (2005). *Prostitution policy: Revolutionizing practice through a gendered perspective.* New York: New York University Press.

Mensah, J., Prempeh, E., and Adjibolosoo, S. (2004). *Globalization and the human factor: Critical insights.* Aldershot, UK: Ashgate.

Monzini, P. (2005). *Sex traffic: Prostitution, crime, and exploitation.* Black Point, NS, Canada: Fernwood.

Moreno, N. (2008, January 17). En Nicaragua aumenta el 15% el índice de explotación sexual infantil. *El Nuevo Diario,* A5.

Mujeres, H. (2007). *Nicaragua. "No más vidas truncadas."* Retrieved September 6, 2008, from http://www.mujereshoy.com/secc_n/3826.shtml

Nokomis Foundation. (2002). *We can do better: Helping prostituted women and girls in Grand Rapids make healthy choices.* <http://www.nokomisfoundation.org/documents/WeCanDoBetter.pdf> (6 Sept. 2008).

OAS. (2003). *Trafficking in women and children: Research findings and follow-up.* Punta Cana, Dominican Republic: Author.

O'Connell, J. (2005). *Children in the global sex trade.* Cambridge, UK: Polity Press.

Pruitt, D., and LaFont, S. (1995) For love and money: Romance tourism in Jamaica. *Annals of Tourism Research, 22*(2), 419–440.

Radcliffe, S. (2001). Development, the state, and transnational political connections: State and subject formation in Latin America. *Global Networks, 1*(1), 19–36.

Reporte de la explotación sexual, comercial de la niñez en Nicaragua. (2005). Managua, Nicaragua.

Review of child labour, education and poverty agenda: Central American country report. (2006). <http://www.globalmarch.org/resourcecentre/PHotos/Central%20America.pdf> (8 Sept. 2008).

Rojas, R. (2007, January). *Diagnostico de ocurrencia del abuso sexual.* Paper presented at the Encuentro nacional contra el abuso sexual, Esteli, Nicaragua.

Sabbagh, D. (2004). *Affirmative action policies: An international perspective.* Retrieved September 6, 2008, from http://hdr.undp.org/en/reports/global/hdr2004/papers/HDR2004_Daniel_Sabbagh.pdf

Sanchez, C. (2007, November 26). OIT advierte sobre explotación sexual infantil. *LaVoz.com.*

Saunders, K. (2002). Introduction: Towards a deconstructive post-development criticism. In K. Saunders (Ed.), *Feminist post-development thought: Rethinking modernity, post-colonialism and representation* (pp. 1–38). London: Zed Books.

Sevilla, S. (2007). OIT advierte sobre la explotación sexual infantil. *LaVoz*.com

Steinberg, J. (2005). The political landscape: Constellations of authority in early complex polities. *American Antropologist, 107*(4), 745–746.

Torres-Saillant, S. (2006). *An intellectual history of the Caribbean.* New York: Palgrave Macmillan.

U.S. State Department. (2005). "Trafficking in persons report released by the office to monitor and combat trafficking in persons" (June 3, 2005). *Trends in Organized Crime, 9*(10), 55–100.

UNICEF. (2003). *At a glance: Nicaragua.* <http://www.unicef.org/infobycountry/nicaragua.html> (6 Sept. 2008).

UNICEF. (2007, July). *Self-evaluation of the institutions in charge of child protection.* Paper presented at the Institutional Self-Evaluation meeting, Santo Domingo, Dominican Republic.

Vos, M. (1999). *The commercial sexual exploitation of children: An overview.* Retrieved <http://www.ecpatusa.org/background.asp> (10 Sept. 2007).

Yashar, D. (2005). *Contesting citizenship in Latin America.* New York: Cambridge University Press.

VII

NORTH AMERICA

Kimberly A. McCabe and Sabita Manian

I N 2004, BALES REPORTED THAT OVER 200,000 individuals were enslaved as prostitutes and that approximately 25 percent of these individuals have been trafficked into the United States for sex work. Poulin (2003) suggested that the reality now facing the United States is that the sex industry is beginning to occupy a central position in the economics of the country. Finally, Hughes, in her 2001 study of sex trafficking within U.S. borders estimated that the United States is increasingly engaged in the sex trafficking of women and children. In response, the United States has been a global leader in the war against human trafficking. From a legal perspective, the United States has provided model legislation and minimum standards to ensure that victimization by the hands of traffickers ends. Canada has also been recognized for its efforts to reduce human trafficking, and Mexico, because of its close ties with the United States, has recently announced that it will also improve efforts to reduce both sex and labor trafficking. However, there are those researchers and government officials that suggests the countries in North America are only scratching the surface of the problem and question the utility of North America's efforts to end this form of victimization when conditions on victims' rights within those conditions are less than desirable. This section provides three chapters—one on the United States, one on Canada, and one on Mexico—in an attempt to discuss efforts to reduce sex trafficking within North America and to identify gaps in implemented actions.

The United States, although responsible for the classification of countries within their established tier system, does not classify itself. The U.S. government acknowledges that its country is a source and destination country for thousands of victims of sex trafficking and placed approximately $27 million in 2006 for domestic anti-trafficking efforts (U.S. Department of State, 2007). The United States prohibits all forms of human trafficking through criminal statutes and all 50 states enforce some sort of legislation prohibiting victimization through trafficking (McCabe, 2008). However, efforts are still required to assure cooperation between the United States and Canada and the United States and Mexico.

Canada is primarily a destination and transit country for sex trafficking. Although border control efforts in Canada have had a significant impact on cases of sex trafficking, efforts to control trafficking within the country have not been focused. Victims in Canada are eligible for assistance in terms of temporary residence in the country although critics claim that the complexity of the process has prevented most victims from requesting assistance (U.S. Department of State, 2004). Canada has been classified as a Tier 1 country because of its efforts to reduce sex trafficking. Law enforcement efforts are standardized, however, limitations exist in terms of efforts to coordinate arrest, prosecution, and conviction.

Mexico's efforts to end sex trafficking are mixed. National commitments are limited as the United States continues to request assistance with cross-border illegal migration. Mexico claims to support ant-trafficking policies to end human trafficking. Mexico has been classified as a Tier 2 country, however, legislative efforts have recently been enacted to reduce sex trafficking; however, little in terms of progress has been made in Mexico to assist victims of sex trafficking.

The three chapters in this section discuss reducing sex trafficking from each country's perspective and controlling sex trafficking as a result of cooperative efforts among the United States, Canada, and Mexico. Despite their efforts to reduce the incidents of human trafficking and the fact that the United States does not rank itself in the tier classification system, all three countries serve as source, transit, or destination countries for victims of sex trafficking.

References

Bales, K. (2004). *New Slavery: A Reference Handbook* (2nd edition). Santa Barbara, CA: ABC News.

Hughes, D. (2001). "The Natasha Trade. Transnational Sex Trafficking." *National Institute of Justice Journal, 246* (January 2001), pp. 9–14.

McCabe, K. (2008). *The Trafficking of Persons: National and International Responses.* NY: Peter Lang.

Poulin, R. (2003). "Globalization and the Sex Trade: Trafficking and the Commodification of Women and Children." *Canadian Woman Studies, 22*(3/4), 36–43.

U.S. Department of State (2004, June). *Trafficking in Persons.* Report. Washington, DC: Office to Monitor and Combat Trafficking in Persons.

U.S. Department of State (2007, June). *Trafficking in Persons.* Report. Washington, DC: Office to Monitor and Combat Trafficking in Persons.

14

Sex Trafficking in the United States

Kimberly A. McCabe

THE UNITED STATES OF AMERICA IS referred to as the land of the free. It is the country of opportunity. It is the country of advancements to ensure a better quality of life. How is the United States also a destination country for sex trafficking? Tiefenbrun (2002) and Miller, Decker, Silverman, and Raj (2007) suggest that approximately 50,000 of women and children are sex trafficked into the United States. The U.S. government reports that the number of individuals sex trafficked into the United States is lower than 50,000 although officials acknowledge that sex trafficking is the most common reason for human trafficking in this country (McCabe, 2008). Experts in the field of sex trafficking suggest that the movement of these victims may be on an individual or group basis and that these movements are usually based on relationships between the traffickers and brothel operators (Richard, 1999) and that victims of sex trafficking have mortality rates 40 times higher than the national average (Chesler, 1994). These victims are exposed to serious health risks such as physical violence and sexually transmitted diseases as well as the conditions related to their confinement (Sulaimanova, 2006).

The reality now facing the United States is that the sex industry now occupies a central position in the development of national and international capitalism and those engineering the sex trafficking of individuals now often occupy some of the highest wealth strata in foreign source countries (Poulin, 2003). In addition and also, not often recognized in cases of sex trafficking in U.S. reports are those victims born in the United

States and trafficked throughout the country without crossing national borders.

It is estimated that profits from sex trafficking may be as high as $12 billion annually following only the criminal activities of drug trafficking and weapons trading. Raymond and Hughes, in their 2001 study of sex trafficking within U.S. borders, estimate the profits at $7 billion annually and suggest that this estimate is conservative as the U.S. population increasingly engages in sex trafficking. As is the case for any sort of human trafficking or organized criminal activity, it is acknowledged that sex trafficking is an activity that does not lend itself to the openness required for accuracy in reporting (Schauer and Wheaton, 2006).

Historical documentation of sex trafficking in the United States is limited; however, it is known that in the 1980s globalization and technology made the movement of victims across national borders much easier. It is also known that organizations to help fight sex trafficking have only existed for about 30 years (Guinn and Steglich, 2003). In this era of civil rights and civil liberties, it is hard for many Americans to believe that sex trafficking can occur and that it does occur within the United States.

Most human trafficking organizations in the United States are small units of one to five individuals who identify, transport, house, and prostitute the victims of sex trafficking (Raymond and Hughes, 2001). However, in some cases of international trafficking into the U.S., larger criminal networks of more than 50 people may be involved (McCabe, 2008). It is noted that although 50 individuals do not prostitute the victims, there are many public and private actors involved in the process of sex trafficking. Thus, the network of recruiters, transporters, and pimps may be quite large, especially when one includes those public actors providing false documents for immigration officials at country borders, those private actors who provide the clients access to the victims, and the public actors (e.g., social service aids, law enforcement officers, and immigration officials) who ignore the criminal activity (Guinn and Steglich, 2003). Just recently the Associated Press (2009) reported that traffickers often place members of their criminal network in the applicant pool for sensitive border protection positions.

In considering the rates by which these international individuals are transported into the United States, Somerset (2004) suggested that both women and children are trafficked throughout Europe and into the United States via Heathrow and Gatwick airports in London or from England, through Scotland, into Canada, and into the United States. In addition, Jalsevac (2006) suggests that Canada also supplies sex trafficking victims for the United States.

Explaining U.S. Sex Trafficking

In attempting to explain how sex trafficking can occur, the explanation can be traced to the founding ideas of Lee's (1966) push–pull theory of migration. Specifically, just as with immigration in general, there are characteristics of a host country that push its natives out and conditions of the destination country that pull the immigrants in. One common method of recruiting women for sex trafficking is by placing an advertisement in local newspapers for nannies or waitresses in the United States. Once the women have been recruited, they are transported to the United States, where their travel documents are confiscated and they are imprisoned by their traffickers and forced to pay off their "debts," which include the costs of their transportation, food, clothing, and shelter (Bell, 2001). The Sun Media (2007) suggests that new victims of sex trafficking may be pimped for up to $10,000 per weekend in the United States, which is definite incentive for those traffickers in the United States.

To increase the likelihood of exploitation, those involved in the day-to-day operations of the mail-order bride business may also be instigators of sex trafficking in the United States. Cullen (2002) reports that mail-order brides often become trapped in an environment of slavery and prostitution. In particular, a young woman who wishes to leave the poverty and inequality of her home country may choose to become a mail-order bride to an American man as American men are increasingly using international matchmaking agencies or mail-order bride catalogs to find a spouse (McCabe, 2008). Unfortunately, though these mail-order bride businesses are considered legitimate, they are essentially unregulated, with neither the brides nor the grooms screened for criminal histories. In 1999, Immigration and Naturalization Services (INS) reported that there were more than 200 mail-order bride agencies operating in the United States and that between 4,000 and 6,000 women were entering the country each year as potential brides. In the last decade, this number has increased (McCabe). Unfortunately for these victims, the love and security of a home are not the outcomes. In fact, these women are often perceived as disposable or replaceable by their new husbands. Mail-order bride brokers are not considered traffickers, but they are regarded as frauds in not disclosing all the facts. These brokers may be liable as traffickers (Miller and Stewart, 1998). The brides who enter the United States for marriage may eventually become slaves.

Spousal prostitution is also related to sex trafficking. McCabe's (2007a) phrase *spousal prostitution* describes the phenomenon of husbands receiving money from individuals in exchange for sex with their wives. In this form of organized prostitution, the husband serves as the pimp for his wife. The wife, lacking the labor skills or education for a profitable occupation within the United States, must engage in prostitution to earn money for her husband's household. Of course, this is not the situation assumed to exist by the young women who agree to become mail-order brides; however, some mail-order brides do become victims of spousal prostitution. Some victims of spousal prostitution are forced to participate in sexual activities by their husbands and moved throughout the country (against their will) to avoid detection and to provide the financial means of survival for their husbands.

The link between prostitution and sex trafficking is always an aspect to consider when attempting to explain sex trafficking. In addition, sex tours and sex rings are often involved with sex trafficking (Brown, 1999). McCabe (2003) uses the phrase *sex ring* to describe a situation in which two or more offenders are simultaneously involved in the sexual exploitation of several victims. The phrase *sex tour* entails the rotation of victims through geographic locations for sexual exploitation. Sex tours are usually thought to exist in locations outside of the United States as it is difficult to believe they also exist within the United States (McCabe, 2008). Sex rings and sex tours are both related to sex trafficking in that victims, for this discussion women and children, are rotated or passed from abuser to abuser; thus, they are victimized repeatedly without the option to end the sexual exploitation.

Finally, emerging entrepreneurs in the area of sexual exploitation are those who utilize film and the Internet. This is the newest avenue for victims of sex trafficking, as often the perpetrators of sex trafficking will "employ" individuals in video production depicting the sexual exploitation of individuals (Taylor and Jamieson, 1999). Of course, these victims receive little or no compensation. Although it is illegal to distribute many of their pornographic and sadistic films over the Internet, law enforcement and Internet service providers (ISPs) rarely monitor these activities, and unless an illegal activity is discovered through a screen by the ISP or a report to law enforcement, the activity continues. In summary, North America, and in particular the United States, is the most reported destination region for sex trafficking (Kangaspunta, 2006). Whether this phenomenon is a result of spousal prostitution, of a decision to seek employment in the United States, or of the mail-order bride industry, the victims of sex trafficking are transported (or smuggled) to the United States and throughout the country for the purpose of sexual activity. Without the English skills to request help from law enforcement or social services, and with the fear of U.S. authorities instilled in them by either their captors or their home country, the victims are forced to participate in sexual exploitation throughout the country.

Offenders

In the United States and other countries, there are two distinct categories of offenders. The first includes those offenders (or traffickers) who make available human beings for sex trafficking—the individuals who recruit (or kidnap) the victims, the individuals who transport those victims to and throughout the United States, and the individuals who foster the sexual abuse of the victims. The second category comprises the customers who pay to abuse the victims. In this category, discussions of offenders must acknowledge their rationale to participate in and pay for sexual exploitation. In the area of sex trafficking, little research exists on anyone other than the victim involved or abused in the sex trafficking, and much of that information is based on very small samples (Raymond, 2004).

In the United States, the sex trafficking of women is primarily accomplished through crime rings and criminal networks. Some of these crime rings are exclusively involved in human trafficking and some are involved in a number of diversified criminal activities (Kangaspunta, 2006). Those involved exclusively in human trafficking are more likely to be organized around a core group (McCabe, 2008). In this organizational structure, a small number of individuals form a relatively tight and structured core group. Around this small core is a larger group of associated individuals and around this group of associated individuals are a larger number of peripheral players. In terms of the organizational structure of criminal networks involving diversified criminal activities, a hierarchically structured organization exists and is characterized by distinct lines of control and responsibility (Kangaspunta, 2006). In this organizational structure, there exists a single leadership structure and a strong sense of identity and responsibilities in terms of criminal actions. Regardless of the structure, there are large, medium, and small criminal networks involved in the sex trafficking of women (Bertone, 2000). Specifically, large-scale networks recruit women in what appear to be legal ways, such as posing as employment agency employees with national and international contacts to identify nannies for work in the United States. The medium-scale networks, thought most often to exist for entry into the United States, traffic women from country to country, and the small-scale organized crime networks traffic women on the basis of requests for certain types of women from brothel owners (Bertone, 2000).

Those involved in sex trafficking work under the same models as drug trafficking or weapons trafficking. Individuals involved in sex trafficking are often identified only through gatekeepers in the industry. Those involved in the trafficking of individuals for sex guard themselves against authorities in immigration, in law enforcement, and in social services. The network of traffickers is quite often small and the leaking of information is unlikely. In larger networks for sex trafficking, members of the organization rarely know all of the players; hence, identification of a large number of specific individuals is unlikely. In fact, in large organizations for sex trafficking, individual members may know only one or two other members (only those with whom they have direct contact); therefore, identification of all of the offenders is impossible (McCabe, 2008). In these conditions, and given the fact that traffickers will resort to extreme violence in controlling their workers and the information obtained through those workers, it is difficult to identify the actual participants within the criminal network (Raymond and Hughes, 2001).

Challenges to Reducing Sex Trafficking in the United States

As with any sort of illegal activity, there are always multiple explanations for the phenomenon. The sex trafficking of individuals is not unique in this respect. Sex trafficking is a multibillion-dollar industry that has what seems to be an endless supply of women ready to be used for profit (Farr, 2004) and consumers in the United States want, and will pay for, exotic bodies from other countries (Poulin, 2003).

Investigative challenge is another aspect fueling the problem of sex trafficking in the United States. Not only are resources limited for law enforcement, but they are also limited for prosecutors, and with little experience in the area of sex trafficking, many prosecutors will attempt to settle cases through pleas instead of trials. As discussed, law enforcement officials rarely receive a report of sex trafficking, and many are unable to distinguish these cases from cases of prostitution; therefore, without the recognition of victims and the victims' willingness to report, sex trafficking continues.

Limited penalties for those convicted of sex trafficking is yet another reason to expect increases in the incidents of sex trafficking in the United States. In comparing a case of human trafficking with a case of drug trafficking, the maximum sentence for slavery is perhaps ten years whereas distributing a kilo of heroin could mean a life sentence (Richard, 1999).

In addition, many of the women who are victims of sex trafficking in the United States did not enter the country legally. Unfortunately, it has been the case that these women were often penalized by immigration officials and removed from the country rather than assisted by social services (Tiefenbrun, 2002).

Finally, one cannot also underestimate the impact of the Internet in the transnational and national trafficking of people for sexual exploitation, as it is not uncommon for traffickers to be found with filming equipment and computers to create and sell pornography (McGinnis, 2004). Researchers are just beginning to recognize the role played by the World Wide Web in the covert or overt advertising of specific sexual services as there exists few systematic approaches to investigating the specific Internet marketplaces of this new cyber-trade (Taylor and Jamieson, 1999).

Many police and governmental organizations are now focusing on the Internet, the World Wide Web, and digital television to identify and pursue cases of sex trafficking (Taylor and Jamieson, 1999). However, with limited law enforcement resources and training to address the Internet and its multiple avenues into criminal activity, cases of sex trafficking via the Internet are also expected to continue, and the number is expected to increase at a much faster rate than the number of law enforcement or governmental regulatory agencies.

The United States is among the top three destinations for sex traffickers globally. Women are trafficked into the sex industry of the United States with promises of lucrative jobs only to be sold into brothels or to strip clubs. Along with Japan and Australia, the United States is the land of victimization for those exploited through sex trafficking.

U.S. Responses to Sex Trafficking

During the twentieth century, there was no single department or agency responsible for collecting data on human trafficking or those offenses relating to trafficking. In 1998, the U.S. government estimated that between 45,000 and 50,000 people were trafficked into the United States annually (U.S. Department of Justice, 2004). Surprisingly, it was not public opinion or human rights groups but big business concerns about labor competition that prompted the awareness of human trafficking in this country (Bales, 2004). Competition and the notion that employers with trafficked employees could complete the work at a fraction of the cost pressed the capitalist system of the United States to begin efforts to eliminate human trafficking. By 2003, the U.S. Department of Justice estimated that between 18,000 and 20,000 individuals were trafficked into the United States.

After Secretary of State Colin Powell announced that monies acquired through human trafficking were used to support the 9/11 hijackers while they lived in this country, public opinion and government efforts began to acknowledge the phenomenon. Legislative and police efforts were initiated to recognize human trafficking as not only a humanitarian interest but also an issue of national security. The 2000 Trafficking Victims Protection Act (hereafter TVPA) established the Office to Monitor and Combat Trafficking in

Persons, in Washington, DC. In February 2002, President Bush signed an Executive Order to establish an Interagency Task Force to include the secretary of state, the attorney general, the secretary of labor, the secretary of health and human services, and the director of the Central Intelligence Agency (CIA). The 2000 TVPA was amended and signed by President George W. Bush in 2003 as the Trafficking Victims Protection Reauthorization Act (TVPRA), which mandated responsibilities and duties regarding human trafficking to federal agencies, including the Department of State, the Department of Labor, and the Department of Health and Human Services.

The TVPRA, signed again in 2005 (H.R. 972), provides tools to combat trafficking in persons both worldwide and domestically. Therefore, in addition to the TVPA's requirements to provide victim assistance, to define new crimes and penalties, and to assist foreign countries in drafting their laws against human trafficking, federal agencies were now sharing the responsibility to reduce and eliminate human trafficking. For example, according to a law passed in September 2002, to better inform women about and protect them against abuse and forced prostitution, foreign-born women may request to view their fiancés' criminal history before leaving their country for the United States (Crandall et al., 2005). Of course, viewing this information is not mandatory, and many women in the mail-order bride industry are not aware this information is available.

Since 2002, the Department of Justice has prosecuted human trafficking offenders, and the Department of Health and Human Services continues to provide medical services, shelter, and counseling to the victims. The Department of Justice's trafficking caseload doubled between 2001 and 2003. According to the Department of State, as of January 2003 approximately 450 trafficking victims had benefited from these newly created provisions. To better inform the public and victims, the departments of Labor, Justice, and Health and Human Services have developed brochures that identify the signs of human trafficking and approximately 200 international anti-trafficking programs have been funded by the United States in countries around the globe (U.S. Department of State, 2004). The U.S. Office to Monitor and Combat Trafficking in Persons annually reports human rights practices with regard to human trafficking by country and hotlines have been established to report victims of human trafficking.

Among its proactive approaches to eliminate human trafficking, the Department of Homeland Security established its Operation Predator program to help protect children from becoming victims of international sex tourism and traffickers and immigration officials warn people about the dangers of purchasing products made by trafficked labor at the land borders of the United States (U.S. Department of State, 2004). The U.S. Department of Justice, in addition to holding its first trafficking-specific training for law enforcement and other federal agencies in June 2004, has continued its training of enforcement officers and supported anti-trafficking task forces in Philadelphia, Atlanta, Phoenix, and other locations throughout the country.

Conclusion

In the United States, the top destinations for sex trafficking are California, New York, Texas, and Las Vegas. The primary source countries for sex trafficking into the United States are Thailand, Vietnam, China, Mexico, Russia, the Ukraine, and the Czech Republic. In most of the documented cases of sex trafficking in the United States, victims are prostituted through force, fraud, or coercion on the part of their traffickers.

Sex trafficking is the result of the conditions of a country of origin as well as the conditions of the country of destination. Specifically, extreme poverty and oppression of women in a country may encourage residents to leave in search of a better life and for an income for their families. Countries with residents who have an existing desire for individuals employed in the sex industry may welcome the victims of sex trafficking for exploitation.

Both men and women are involved in the trafficking of humans for sexual exploitation. Most research supports the idea that the majority of the traffickers are male; however, researchers may soon change their conclusions about the gender of offenders, as more and more women are becoming involved as recruiters, transporters, or brothel madams. Critical in the definition of sex trafficking is that it occurs without the consent of the victim. In addition, the victims of sex trafficking often do not possess the language skills or the trust in U.S. law enforcement required to help them if they decide to end the exploitation. Without the ability to end the abuse, many victims of sex trafficking continue to suffer until they die or are killed.

Finally, sex trafficking is a profitable enterprise, with estimates of annual profits in the millions of dollars. This profit from sex trafficking has historically come with very few negative consequences if it is discovered by law enforcement; hence, for all involved, sex trafficking appears to be a phenomenon that will only increase in the United States.

References

Associated Press. (August 10, 2009). "Point of Corruption More Border Agents Busted." *The News and Advance*, Lynchburg, Virginia, A2.

Bales, K. (2004). *New Slavery: A Reference Handbook* (2nd edition). Santa Barbara, CA: ABC-CLIO.

Bell, R. (2001). Sex Trafficking: A Financial Crime Perspective. *Journal of Financial Crime*, 9 (2), 165–172.

Bertone, A. (2000). International Political Economy and the Politics of Sex. *Gender Issues*, 18 (1), 4–22.

Brown, H. (1999). Sex Crimes and Tourism in Nepal. *International Journal of Contemporary Hospitality Management*, 11 (23), 107–110.

Chesler, P. (1994). "A Woman's Right to Self Defense: The Case of Aileen Carol Wuornos." In *Patriarchy Notes of an Expert Witness*, pp. 11–13. Monroe, MN: Common Courage.

Crandall, M., Senturia, K., Sullivan, M., and Shiu-Thornton, S. (2005). No Way Out: Russian-Speaking Women's Experiences with Domestic Violence. *Journal of Interpersonal Behavior*, 20 (8), 941–958.

Cullen, S. (2002). The Miserable Lives of Mail Order Brides. *Women in Action*, 3, 6–9.

Farr, K. (2004). *Sex Trafficking: The Global Market in Women and Children*. New York: W. H. Freedman.

Guinn, D., and Steglich, E. (2003). *In Modern Bondage: Sex Trafficking in America*. Herndon, VA: Transnational.

Jalsevac, J. (2006). U.S. report soft-pedaling on Germany, Canada sex trafficking say anti-trafficking experts. Life Site News. <www.lifesite.net/ldn/2006/june/06060606.html> (20 June 2007).

Kangaspunta, K. (2006, April). *Trafficking in Persons: Global Patterns*. Vienna, Austria: United Nations Office on Drugs and Crime.

Lee, E. (1966). A Theory of Migration. *Demography*, 1, 47–57.

McCabe, K. (2003). *Child Abuse and the Criminal Justice System*. New York: Peter Lang.

McCabe, K. (2007). Spousal Prostitution. In N. Jackson's (Ed), *Encyclopedia of Domestic Violence*, pp. 673–674, New York: Routledge.

McCabe, K. (2008). *The Trafficking of Persons: National and International Responses*. New York: Peter Lang.

McGinnis, E. (2004). The Horrifying Reality of Sex Trafficking. Washington, DC: Concerned Women for America. December 12. <http://www.cwfa.org> (12 Nov. 2006).

Miller, E., Decker, M., Silverman, J., and Raj, A. (2007). "Migration, Sexual Exploitation, and Women's Health. A Case Report from a Community Health Center." *Violence Against Women*, 13(5), 486–499.

Miller, J., and Stewart, A. (1998). Report from the Roundtable on the Meaning of Trafficking in Persons: A Human Rights Perspective. *Women's Rights Law Reporter*, 20 (1), 1–12.

Poulin, R. (2003). Globalization and the Sex Trade: Trafficking and the Commodification of Women and Children. *Canadian Woman Studies*, 22 (3/4), 38–43.

Raymond, J. (2004). The Impact of the Sex Industry in the EU. Testimony before the European Parliament, January 2004. European Union.

Raymond, J., and Hughes, D. (2001). *Sex Trafficking of Women in the United States: International and Domestic Trends*. Amherst, MA: Coalition Against Trafficking in Women.

Richard, A. (1999, November). *International Trafficking in Women to the United States: A Contemporary Manifestation of Slavery and Organized Crime.* DCI Exceptional Intelligence Analyst Program of Intelligence Monograph. Washington, DC: Center for the Study of Intelligence.

Schauer, E., and Wheaton, E. (2006). Sex Trafficking into the United States: A Literature Review. *Criminal Justice Review,* 31 (2), 146–153.

Somerset, C. (2004). *Cause for Concern?* London: ECPAT.

Sulaimanova, S. (2006). Trafficking in Women from the Former Soviet Union for the Purpose of Sexual Exploitation. In K. Beeks and D. Amir (Eds.), *Trafficking and the Global Sex Industry,* pp. 61–76. Lanham, MD: Lexington Books.

Sun Media. (November 11, 2007). "Social Networking Sites Used for Human Trafficking." <http://www.edmontonsun.com/News/Edmonton/2007/11/11/pf-4648414.html> (28 Jan. 2009).

Taylor, I., and Jamieson, R. (1999). Sex Trafficking and the Mainstream of Market Culture. *Crime, Law, and Social Change,* 32 (3), 257–278.

Tiefenbrun, S. W. (2002). Sex Sells but Drugs Don't Talk: Trafficking of Women Sex Workers and an Economic Solution. *Thomas Jefferson Law Review,* 24 (2), 161–189.

U.S. Department of State. (2004). *Recent Developments in US Government Efforts to End Human Trafficking.* Washington, DC: Office to Monitor and Combat Trafficking in Persons.

15

Sex Trafficking in Canada: Limited Efforts in Law Enforcement

James B. Grassano and T. A. Ryan

THROUGHOUT THE LAST FIVE YEARS of the *Trafficking in Persons Report*, Canada has been placed in the Tier 1 category indicating full compliance with the minimum standards of the Trafficking Victims Protection Act. However, further examinations by U.S. Department of State (2008) and a review of the progress in developing countries (Vanderheyden, 2006) suggest few advancements in recent years in terms of law enforcement efforts within the country focused on arresting those involved in sex trafficking and providing assistance to those victims of sex trafficking (VST).

With borders on the Atlantic and Pacific Oceans, Canada's proximity to the United States facilitates its exchanges with the U.S. and, in many cases, the two countries experience the same sort of criminal problems to include the problem of sex trafficking. Canada is a source, transit, and destination country for sex trafficking; therefore, its role in sex trafficking varies by victim circumstances. Many of the young VSTs are children from Canada and are either runaways or were taken from their families. Many of these victims remain within Canadian borders and some are trafficked to the United States for sexual exploitation. Oftentimes the VSTs are used in sex rings or in sex tours with individuals, including Americans, visiting Canada for the opportunity to participate in forced sex.

Historically, Canada's VSTs have been women and children either from Asia or Eastern Europe; however, that is not the case today. Specifically, there appears to be a clearer separation of nationalities being trafficked to certain areas of Canada with the women and children from Asia being trafficked to Vancouver and/or Western Canada and the women and children from Eastern Europe and Latin America being trafficked to Toronto and/or Eastern Canada. In addition, victims from South Korea as well as victims from other parts of the world are trafficked through Canada to the United States. McCabe (2008) and Somerset (2004) suggested that both women and children may be trafficked via Heathrow and Gatwick airports in London, through Scotland and into Canada, while some VSTs are then trafficked further into the United States. As is the case with many forms of organized crime, when regulatory agents minimize their capacities to control violation, they often contribute to the activity. Law enforcement officers are the first component in the criminal justice system with the opportunity to reduce sex trafficking; however, without the efforts to end sex trafficking by the police, the criminal activity continues. As Canadian law enforcement efforts fail to drastically reduce the problem of human trafficking, sex trafficking increases.

In Canada, there are three levels of law enforcement: municipal, provincial, and federal with most urban areas given the authority by their jurisdictions to maintain their own police forces. Canadian police forces include, but are not limited to, the Royal Canadian Mounted Police (often referred to as the Mounties), the Ontario Provincial Police, and the Quebec Provincial Police. Just as is the case in the various states within the United States, Canadian police forces are often independently operated departments with responsibilities to the laws and ordinances within their jurisdictions. These departments may be responsible for the enforcement of the same laws; however, the lines of jurisdiction do clearly provide separation and, in many cases, may hinder communications among the various police forces. In the United States where communications are often limited by state jurisdictions, information on cases of violence in California may be slow in reaching police departments in Georgia. In Canada, with similar jurisdictional restrictions, information on cases in Montreal may not be immediately released to police forces in Quebec. In addition, just as the Spanish to English barriers in the United States provide problems in communications, Canada has the tradition of English in some police jurisdictions and French in other jurisdictions; thus, a similar problem. Without open communications across police forces and Canada's provincials, information to law enforcement officers on crimes to include sex trafficking may be limited and may not be communicated.

From a legal standpoint, Canada prohibits all forms of human trafficking through its Criminal Code, which was amended in 2005 to include specific actions symptomatic of sex trafficking and penalties of up to 14 years in prison for those convicted of trafficking. However, reports suggest that human trafficking criminal enterprises have operated in Western Canada for at least 20 years and for decades longer in central Canada; hence today these networks utilized in sex trafficking are more sophisticated than ever (Sun Media, 2007). To address transnational trafficking, Canada's Immigration and Refugee Protection Act was enacted; however, law enforcement outcomes of arrest of those persons involved in human trafficking have been minimal. One explanation for this inactivity is lack of concern; however, the most plausible explanations for the lack of police outcomes are related to detection in the elements of the crime of sex trafficking and police discretion.

As research suggests, sex trafficking is linked with prostitution and/or pornography (McCabe, 2008). Although Canada has historically taken a stand against prostitution, it does exist within the Canadian borders and its related activities fuel sex trafficking. Legitimate businesses such as massage parlors and escort services serve as fronts for those traffickers targeting individuals for sexual exploitation. Canadian law enforcement officials routinely arrest women for prostitution to simply see them returned to the streets after 24 hours. This cycle of detention, arrest, detention, re-arrest is often viewed by law enforcement officers as never ending and without reason; therefore, many police officers, after several encounters with individuals they have identified as prostitutes, will not continue to arrest these persons. The less serious a law enforcement officer perceives a crime is to the public, the more likely the officer will use police discretion and ignore the criminal activity (Cole and Smith, 2005). Legal authorities provide law enforcement officers the power to deprive people of their liberties, to arrest individuals, and to use force to control the actions of individuals (Cole and Smith). For many police officers, prostitution is viewed as a victimless crime and their legal authorities also provide law enforcement the power to do nothing. Unfortunately for VSTs, quite often their activity is viewed by police officers as consensual prostitution and therefore those individuals organizing the sex trafficking network are not likely to be aggressively targeted for arrest by the officers. Without the detection of the VSTs, there is no hope in identifying their traffickers.

One of the newest enterprises for those involved in the trafficking of individuals for sexual exploitation involves the internet and pornography (McCabe, 2008). Taylor and Jamieson (1999) documented the use of victims of sex trafficking in the production of pornography to be distributed electronically; however, without police involvement in controlling this crime the activity continues (Vaughan, 1992). As law enforcement officers and Internet Service Providers rarely monitor the distribution of pornography via the internet (McCabe, 2007), and as most police forces have few if any personnel dedicated

to monitoring the internet, the detection of VSTs in the production of pornography is unlikely. Unfortunately, the use of child victims for the production of child pornography does little to increase police efforts toward arrest in
this area (McCabe, 2003). Without the efforts and arrests by Canada's police
forces, the process to reduce sex trafficking does not occur. During 2007 and
2008, arrests in cases of sex trafficking were minimal although some suggest
Canada has as many as 15,000 victims of sex trafficking and it has recently
been reported that girls were being sold in Montreal for approximately $2,000
(Womensphere, 2008). Instead of funding law enforcement efforts, Canadian
authorities have placed more of its resources into public awareness.

Specifically, Canada has designed and implemented various anti-trafficking
media campaigns and victim services are available throughout most police
jurisdictions. To specifically address the problem of child victims of sex trafficking, Canada's *Cybertip.com* has existed since 2002 as an online tip line
dedicated to raising public awareness on child trafficking. Cybertip.com published information on the top five risks children face while using the internet
as well as signs of child sexual exploitation. It is suggested that Cybertip.com
has led to the identification of more that 15,000 websites intended to victimize
children (ECPAT, 2007).

In 2007, the Canadian government funded and distributed anti-trafficking
brochures to educate the public on sex trafficking and the resources available
to victims of sex trafficking. Also in 2007, British Columbia's provincial government opened a human trafficking office to improve the coordination of
cases between NGOs and law enforcement and most Canadian jurisdictions
now provide some services to VSTs.

Victims' rights in Canada are usually supported and individuals victimized
by sex traffickers are not held responsible for their actions. In 2008, the Canadian government provided $5 million to help address the limited funds from
NGOs to assist victims. Currently, Canada's federal officials are working with
Vancouver's Police force to establish measures to prevent sex trafficking during the 2010 Winter Olympics (U.S. Department of State, 2008).

In summary, Canada is a source, transit, and destination country for sex
trafficking. Similar to the United States, Canada has experienced many of the
same problems with the detection of human trafficking cases and the prosecution of traffickers; however, government efforts maintain a desire to end this
criminal activity. The Canadian government fully complies with the standards
for the elimination of human trafficking and Canada's anti-trafficking awareness plans continue to increase; however, law enforcement efforts are minimal.
Through training of law enforcement personnel to distinguish victims of sex
trafficking from willing prostitutes, Canada's police forces may further impact
Canada's goal to eliminate human trafficking.

References

Cole, G., and Smith, C. (2005). *Criminal Justice in America* (4th ed.). Belmont, CA: Wadsworth.

ECPAT. (2007). *Info ECPAT*. ECPAT Groups Monthly Newsletter, March 20, p.4. Washington, DC: ECPAT.

McCabe, K. (2008). *The Trafficking of Persons: National and International Responses*. NY: Peter Lang.

McCabe, K. (2007). The Role of Internet Service Providers in Cases of Child Pornography and Child Prostitution. *Social Science Computer Review, 25*(2), 1–5.

McCabe, K. (2003). *Child Abuse and the Criminal Justice System*. NY: Peter Lang.

Somerset, C. (2004). *Cause for Concern?* London: ECPAT.

Sun Media. (November 11, 2007). Social Networking Sites Used for Human Trafficking: Hundreds of Albertans Get Targeted Each Year. <www.edmontonsun.com/News/Edmonton/2007/11/11/pf-4648414.html> (10 Jan. 2009).

Taylor, I., and Jamieson, R. (1999). Sex Trafficking in the Mainstream Market Culture. *Crime, Law, and Social Change, 32*(3), 257–278.

U.S. Department of State. (2008). *Trafficking in Persons*. Report. Washington, DC: Office to Monitor and Combat Trafficking in Persons.

Vanderheyden, T. (2006, March 2). *Canada an International Embarrassment on Sex Trafficking*. Lifesitenews.com. Accessed at <http://www.lifesitenews.com> (28 Jan. 2009).

Vaughan, D. (1992). The Macro-micro Connection in White-Collar Crime Theory." K. Schlegel and D. Weisburd (Eds.) *White Collar Crime Reconsidered*. Boston: Northeastern University.

Womensphere. (2008, April 16). "Rise in Human Trafficking Largely Unnoticed in Canada." *Womensphere*. <http://womensphere.wordpress.com> (2 March 2009).

16

Sex Trafficking and Mexico

David H. Richards

THE UNITED STATES CONSIDERS Mexico a Tier 2 state, or a "country whose government does not fully comply with the TVPA's minimum standards, but is making significant efforts to bring itself into compliance with those standards." (U.S. Department of State, 2009). Due to this seeming negligence by Mexico, this country has been for years (2000–2003 and 2008–2009) listed as Tier 2. They did, however, slip in their rankings to Tier 2 Watch List for four consecutive years (2004–2007) for not presenting evidence of adequate commitment to prevent human trafficking. The United States sees Mexico's handling of the human trafficking issue as lacking, a problem with security dimensions for both countries.

One infamous example of the kind of trafficking that occurs between Mexico and the United States can be found in the case of "Rosa," a woman who testified to the U.S. Congress in 2000 as part of a hearing on Human Trafficking. Her story of being smuggled across the border into the United States to get a better job to help her family ended with her being held in various trailer park brothels as an involuntary sex worker, often servicing multiple men a day. She was thirteen years old at the time. (Merida, 2002). Although stories like this are tragic, to fully understand Mexico's trafficking situation and apparent lack of prosecutorial effort, the state's situation should be placed in context. Mexico faces three significant problems when it comes to dealing with trafficking of persons: it shares a fairly porous border with the United States, itself a destination for many trafficked persons from all over the world. It faces large levels of poverty compared to its neighbors in the north yet offers a relatively higher standard of living compared to neighbors in the south. This leads to a large pool of people desperate for economic opportunity and a growing influx of its own immigrants who are easy prey for traffickers. Lastly, the country suffers from high levels of corruption from the local level up to the federal government level, making it easier for traffickers, who are often tied to the larger issue of the drug trade in the country, to conduct business.

Mexico is of particular interest to the United States for two reasons: as a border state, Mexico is a large source of trafficked persons and Mexico itself is a destination for many trafficked people from Central and South America, many of whom never make it as far north as the United States. Additionally, people from outside the hemisphere are often taken first to Mexico and then trafficked across the U.S.-Mexican border. These factors make Mexico a significant source and destination for trafficked persons in the world (U.S. State Department 2008, Landesman 2004).

The United States has a unique relationship with Mexico. It shares a long border which has been the source not only of trafficked persons but also large numbers of legal and illegal immigrants. This presents a tricky situation between the two countries. The United States benefits from cheap labor from Mexico, and Mexico benefits from sending labor abroad and receiving remittances in return. Thus, efforts to stem cross-border migration are often not entirely successful. To further complicate matters, Mexico is a major transshipment point for illegal narcotics brought into the United States. Drug traffic is often commingled with human traffic, making the problem more difficult. Mexicans caught illegally crossing the U.S. border are almost always returned (Martin and Miller 2000). They usually do this voluntarily since prosecution by the United States might lead to a jail term. This makes it more difficult to sort out persons who might be victims of trafficking. As one report on trafficking noted, prosecution of cross-border traffickers is difficult since their victims often "get up and walk away" (Martin and Miller, 2000, 969).

Although a large number of people, especially Central Americans (whose status in Mexico may be illegal to begin with), end up in forced labor or sex trade within Mexico, the majority end up in the United States. This means that the problem becomes, in essence, a U.S. problem and no longer a Mexican problem.

Connected with trafficking in Mexico is the drug trade. This trade has been the focus of intense efforts by the Mexican and U.S. governments. Although trafficked people often act as mules to carry drugs into the United States and once there they are often forced into prostitution or other forced labor by the drug runners, the focus of the United States and now Mexico has been mostly on narcotic interdiction. Dealing with trafficked persons becomes something of a secondary issue. Clearly the two are connected, and any attempts to deal with the drug trade will impact the trafficking, but trafficking is not the focus of either governments' law enforcement efforts at this time.

Closely connected with the drug trade are the trafficking "families" who control the trafficking trade much in the same way that a small number of groups control the drug trade. "Los Lenones" are family structured groups that frequently deal multiple women at the same time, often in connection with similar organized crime groups in the United States. Although a common tactic is to offer a promise of jobs in "El Norte" many young women are simply kidnapped by members of the family. Payoffs to local law enforcement in Mexico are widespread to the point that federal agents within the Mexican government must often fight not only with the Los Lenones but also local police (Landesman, 2004).

The kinds of people trafficked into and through Mexico mirror trends elsewhere but have some different categories such as people from other third world nations. Many are children, both girls and boys. Many women are also exploited. Mexico is also a place where men are exploited for labor as well. The persistent issue of poverty in Mexico adds to this equation. About half of the people in Mexico live below the UN poverty line (World Bank, 2008). This creates a large pool of desperate people seeking economic opportunity, even if that opportunity seems fraught with risk. It should be noted that the problem with most of the human trafficking done out of Mexico is that those who are trafficked almost never actually make money. In most situations the women and children forced in sex work were not paid (Bode, 2005; Landesman, 2004; Marzulli, 2005; Merida, 2002.) These cases should be seen very differently from possible cases of voluntary participation in prostitution.

Somewhat unique to Mexico are the fairly large number of minors who are sent through Mexico from Central America on their way to meet up with family in the United States. In recent years some of these children have fallen victim to traffickers before they were able to reach the United States. Mexico also has a large number of emigrants seeking entry into the United States, making them vulnerable to exploitation. As mentioned earlier, in many cases what may be seen as exploitation may in fact be a more subtle form of smuggling payoff. The line between the two is often very blurred.

Mexico also has a significant internal human trafficking problem. Immigrants from the rest of the Americas (especially Central America) often end up in Mexico as sex workers. Traffickers within Mexico prefer people from outside Mexico since they are often illegal immigrants or separated from their normal social support network. Both of these conditions, coupled with the high levels of poverty, make for a large pool from which traffickers can pick. Caribbean and Central American women are seen as being especially desirable in the sex trade within Mexico (U.S. State Department). And while there is local demand, many end up servicing tourists in one of the many Mexican resort areas or in the U.S. border area (Bode, 2005). It is this internal trade that Mexico's local state governments have focused on more than transshipment to the United States. Local prosecution levels are much lower than federal levels. Most of these cases are for local forced labor and, to a lesser extent, the sex trade. This does not mean that there is less of a problem with local sex trade, but that women and children in the sex trade are less likely to come forward with complaints, especially because Mexican law demands charges from the victim to proceed in prosecution.

Mexico has recognized the problem of human trafficking in recent years as trafficking has grown. By 2008, most states within Mexico had passed anti-trafficking laws. Similar laws that had been passed in 2007 were put into effect on the federal level in early 2009. The U.S. State Department has not found any local level prosecution of traffickers, while only 24 federal cases had been brought by the end of 2008. This, in a country where the government itself estimates there are at least 20,000 children trafficked each year, and up to three times as many adults. (U.S. State Department, 2009; Godoy, 2008)

Mexican law on trafficking is fairly tough but not effectively enforced. Sentences range from six to twelve years, half again for public officials who are convicted under the 2007 law. However, victims must press charges, forcing the exploited to come forward. This has led to few cases being brought forward on the federal level and even fewer on the state level. Additionally, corruption at most levels in the Mexican government (Montinola and Jackman, 2002; Seligson, 2002) means that most traffickers are protected by the very system meant to prosecute them. Transparency International ranks Mexico as 72nd in its corruption index, in the top half of the most corrupt nations (Corruption Perceptions Index 2008). Reports of police who turn the other way, or even protect traffickers as they solicit customers are common (Bode, 2005). Customs officers at Mexican airports often help traffickers process in women and children from outside Mexico (Landesman, 2004). Most victims are poor and undereducated, making it difficult for them to press charges if allegations are made and because of government corruption, victims are fearful of retaliation.

One bright spot in Mexico is the government's "Operation Limpieza" which is aimed at corruption within the government. This program, started in 2008, has successfully prosecuted midlevel government bureaucrats, however, often the charges are not related directly to trafficking (U.S. State Department, 2009). The Mexican government routinely treats smuggling of illegal immigrants and trafficking as the same thing. Particularly in Mexico the line between the two is often difficult to distinguish. People who are smuggled into the United States often end up working under forced labor conditions or as sex workers to pay off the *coyotes* who brought them to the United States.

Many of the officials caught in Operation Limpieza are convicted on smuggling charges or lesser corruption charges.

Mexico does not have a good system for helping victims of trafficking even when they are found, especially if those victims are foreign nationals. Persons, especially in the sex trade, who are not Mexican, are generally deported within 90 days; this, despite problems of retribution or even imprisonment once they are returned. Mexican law does allow for persons who cooperate with the police in arresting traffickers to stay in the country on a one year visa, but in 2008 only three individuals met these criteria (U.S. Department of State, 2009). Even for its own citizens Mexico has been slow to provide government help to victims. There are only two facilities in the entire country set up to rehabilitate victims. Most work has been done by nongovernmental agencies, such as Covenant House (http://www.covenanthouse.org/) (U.S. Department of State, 2009). There have been several shelters built for victims of trafficking but the number of beds available in these shelters is still under 100, in a country with well over 100 million people (Marzulli, 2005).

As a developing democracy, Mexico faces many problems that such states must deal with: economic development, providing basic services such as education, clean water and healthcare and building up infrastructure. This means that issues like human trafficking, (which despite its widespread nature, actually affects only a small part of the population) is pushed to the side. When it comes to going after sex traffickers specifically in Mexico, several obstacles present themselves in particular: large sectors of the Mexican citizenry live below the poverty line making them easy marks for traffickers. A closely connected drug trade, fueled by internal and U.S. demand, is widespread and corruption exists in every level of the government. These three factors not only impede prosecution of traffickers, but also lead to an environment where there are both people to traffic and an opportunity to do so. Mexico represents a case in which all the elements present make dealing with the problem of trafficking seemingly insurmountable as evidenced by its lack of progress in moving out of the Tier 2 category in the past decade.

References

Bode, N. (2005). "From the Mean Streets of Mexico to the Sad Streets of Queens," *Daily News New York,* April 3 2005.

Godoy, E. (2008). "16,000 Victims of Child Sexual Exploitation," IPS, Inter Press News Agency, <http://www.ipsnews.net/news.asp?idnews=38872> (20 July 2009).

Landesman, P. (2004). "The Girls Next Door," *The New York Times,* January 25, 2004.

Martin, P., and Miller, M. (2000). "Smuggling and Trafficking: A Conference Report," *International Migration Review,* Vol. 34(3): 969–975.

Marzulli, J. (2005). "Dirty Little Secret in Corona. Cops Allege Homes in Queens Were Prisons for Latin Sex Slaves" *Daily News (New York)*, April 4, 2005.

Merida, K. (2002). "Of Human Bondage; From Her Desk, It's Easy to See that Slavery Isn't Yet History," *The Washington Post*, April 7, 2002 Sunday.

Montinola, G., and Jackman, R. (2002). "Sources of Corruption: A Cross-Country Study," *British Journal of Political Science*, Vol. 32, No. 1 (Jan., 2002): 147–170.

Seligson, M. (2002). "The Impact of Corruption on Regime Legitimacy: A Comparative Study of Four Latin American Countries," *The Journal of Politics*, Vol. 64, No. 2 (May, 2002): 408–433.

Transparency International. (2008). "Corruption Perceptions Index." <http://www.transparency.org/policy_research/surveys_indices/cpi/2008/faq> (14 July 2009).

United States Department of State. (2008). *Trafficking in Persons Report 2008*—Mexico, June 2008.

United States Department of State. (2009). *Trafficking in Persons Report 2009*—Mexico, June 2009.

World Bank. (2008). "Poverty in Mexico—Fact Sheet." <http://go.worldbank.org/MDXERW23U0> (16 July 2009).

17

Conclusion:
Anti-Trafficking Efforts

Kimberly A. McCabe and Sabita Manian

GLOBAL ESTIMATES OF HUMAN trafficking range from four million to 600,000 victims each year (IOM, 2009). The majority of those individuals are victims of *sex* trafficking—revealing the difficulty in data gathering and accountability. Currently, the U.S. State Department estimates suggest that approximately 70 percent of the victims of sex trafficking are female and approximately 50 percent of the victims are under the age of 18. Victims of sex trafficking may be forced into prostitution, pornography, prostitution for the military or militia, spousal prostitution, and prostitution for the sex-tourism industry.

Many nations have either misunderstood the definition of human trafficking or failed to comprehend the magnitude of incidents of trafficking that have occurred within their own geographical borders. The United Nations has defined *human trafficking* as "the recruitment, transfer, harboring or receipt of persons by threat or use of force." This definition is similar to that used by the U.S. State Department's Trafficking Victims Protection Act of 2000 (henceforth TVPA) which describes severe forms of trafficking as: "(a) sex trafficking in which a commercial sex act is induced by force, fraud, or coercion, or in which the person induced to perform such an act has not attained 18 years of age; or (b) the recruitment, harboring, transportation, provision, or obtaining of a person for labor or services, through the use of force, fraud, or coercion for the purpose of subjection to involuntary servitude, peonage, debt bondage, or slavery" (U.S. Department of State, 2008).

In 2000, with nearly 700,000 individuals trafficked annually, the majority of whom are women and children, the United States Congress passed the *Victims of Trafficking and Violence Protection Act of 2000, P.L. 106–386,* also known as the *Trafficking Victims Protection Act* (TVPA). The TVPA mandated that the U.S. Secretary of State submit a report on "severe forms of trafficking in persons" to Congress, by June 1 (Trafficking in Persons Report, 2001). As prescribed by the TVPA, the State Department produces an annual report which identifies countries in a tier classification system as a measure of their efforts to reduce human trafficking.

When the U.S. Congress passed the TVPA in October 2000, they made an attempt to provide a comprehensive definition of trafficking and to address the issues relating to human trafficking on the national and international levels. After the 2000 TVPA, as cases of human trafficking in the United States and abroad became more prevalent, more legislation was enacted by the Clinton administration. In 2003 President George W. Bush signed the amended *Trafficking Victims Protection Reauthorization Act* (TVPRA), which further strengthened the U.S. government's response to human trafficking by recognizing the needs of the victims of human trafficking. In 2005, the TVPRA was reinforced with proclamations of the United States' support to end this activity and a new phrase, "severe forms of trafficking," was adopted. Thus, the category of *severe forms of trafficking* is expected to include the recruitment, harboring, and so on of a person under one of the following three conditions: (1) human trafficking for labor, (2) human trafficking for commercial sex acts, and (3) human trafficking of those under the age of 18. It is also important to note that through this change in legislation a child under the age of 18 (regardless of country of origin) cannot give his or her consent to be moved from one country to another; thus, a specific type of human trafficking— child trafficking—is identified. In addition, the parent or guardian of the child cannot give consent to the trafficker of that child for his or her movement for the purposes of forced labor or sexual exploitation (UNODC, 2006).

This text explored the variants of human sex trafficking for Commercial Sexual Exploitation (CSE) from a global perspective in terms of its multiple purposes and its victims. The approach was multidisciplinary with scholars from the fields of law, sociology, criminology, history and political science presenting their analyses through the lenses of their respective disciplines. Chapters provided an assessment of human sex trafficking in geographical regions as categorized by the U.S. State Department's Annual Report on Trafficking in Persons 2008. Geographical regions were: Africa, East Asia and the Pacific region, Europe, the Near East, South Asia, the Western Hemisphere, and North America.

As the chapters in the text revealed, while each case of sex trafficking in each region of the world is unique in its own way, there are some common realities that one encounters in the sex trafficking of women and children for commercial sexual purposes. First, the politics of numbers and the quantification itself present a problematic that is not easily resolved. The U.S. State Department's data gathering often are based on information provided by one or two local nongovernmental organizations, when government information may not be forthcoming or sometimes may supplement the host government's documentation. Second, certain social issues that are common include the devaluing of women and the personification of women as objects, gender inequity as well as global inequalities, a material culture that constantly provides the myth of glamour and allure that forces girls and women to seek what appears to be a path to fulfillment. Third, while conflict situations exacerbate the prevalence of trafficking for CSE, non–conflict related venues for sports and entertainment also tend to aggravate trafficking incidences.

Trafficking in people is now considered the third most profitable activity for organized crime as there are more and more cases of individuals being held against their will either for labor or for sex. Since 2002, the U.S. Department of Justice has prosecuted sex trafficking offenders and the Department of Health and Human Services continues to provide medical services, shelter, and counseling to victims of sex trafficking. To better inform the public, the U.S. Departments of Labor, Justice, and Health and Human Services have developed brochures for nongovernmental organizations (NGOs) to distribute to help identify victims of sex trafficking and over 200 international anti-trafficking programs have been funded in countries around the world (McCabe, 2008). On the international front, there have been multiple efforts to reduce sex trafficking to include NGOs such as the Global Survival Network and Human Rights Watch and the International Labour Organization's commitment to provide assistance to child victims of sex trafficking (Munro, 2006).

Among the problems that must be acknowledged when addressing human trafficking is the definition itself. Other problems include that there has been no method for collecting information on cases and that the involvement of children as victims of human trafficking is often not recognized nor is there a single department or agency in the world responsible for collecting data on human trafficking or those offenses related to trafficking. The 1948 Universal Declaration of Human Rights states that all human beings are born free, that no one shall be held in slavery or servitude, and that everyone has the right to freedom of movement and to free choice of employment; however, human trafficking violates these most basic of rights. Finally, the trafficking of humans for sex is a problem that touches every country in one respect or another. Victims of sex trafficking are men, women, and children. These victims are forced through either physical violence or threats of violence to provide sexual services for the profit of their traffickers. This text detailed sex trafficking from a global perspective.

References

International Organization for Migration (IOM). (2009). *N General Assembly Thematic Dialogue: Taking Collective Action to End Human Trafficking.* New York: UN Headquarters, May 2009. <www.un.org/ga/president/63/interactive/ht/iom.pdf> (2 May 2009).

McCabe, K. (2008). *The Trafficking of Persons: National and International Responses.* NY: Peter Lang.

Munro, V. (2006). "Stopping Traffic? A Comparative Study of Responses to the Trafficking of Women for Prostitution." *British Journal of Criminology, 46*(2), 318–333.

U.S. Department of State. 2001. *Trafficking in Persons Report.* <www.state.gov/g/tip/rls/tiprpt/2001/3929.htm> (2 May 2008).

U.S. Department of State. (2008, June). *Trafficking in Persons.* Report. Washington, DC: Office to Monitor and Combat Trafficking in Persons.

United Nations Office on Drugs and Crime (UNODC). (2006, April). *Trafficking in Persons: Global Patterns.* UN: Human Trafficking Unit.

Index

About the Contributors

Dr. Karin Bruckmüller is university assistant at the Department for Criminal Law and Criminology at the University of Vienna (Austria) and honorary employee to the Austrian Victim Support Organisation "Weisser Ring"; her research topics are preventing and combating trafficking in human beings, victims' rights and victimology, criminal sanctions and alternatives to imprisonment, juvenile justice system, and medical criminal law.

Dr. Brad Bullock is professor and chair of sociology at Randolph College. He has a Ph.D. in Sociology from Vanderbilt University. His wide interests include international development, political economy, and the Caribbean. He is co-author of "Globalization's Gendered Consequences for the Caribbean," forthcoming in *Eternal Colonialism* (2010). Currently, he is working on a book-length manuscript on the Caribbean.

Michael A. Bush is a country manager for Xe in Tampa, Florida. Mr. Bush, a former law enforcement officer and trainer of law enforcement in Afghanistan, has received degrees from the University of North Carolina at Wilmington (BA) and the University of South Carolina (MCJ). His research interests include police training, police policy, and terrorism. Mr. Bush continues to provide training support to law enforcement in Afghanistan and other Middle Eastern countries.

Dr. Mirna Carranza is an assistant professor at the School of Social Work, McMaster University, Ontario, Canada. Her research interests include immigrant and refugee families and their process of acculturation as family units, which are topics of her forthcoming publications that include, "Surviving War and Trauma" in D. S. Silva (Ed.), *Latina & Chicana Mothering;* "Cross-border Family Therapy: An Innovative Approach with Latin American Refugee Women in Canada," in *Journal of Women in Therapy.* Other publications included "Therapeutic interventions to domestic violence with immigrant couples" in J. Hamel et al., *Interventions in Family Violence: A Casebook* (2008).

Dr. Yingyu Chen is currently an LL.M. candidate at the Washington College of Law, American University. She was a postdoctoral researcher in the Social Science Research Center at the National Science Council in Taiwan and a part-time lead researcher at Taipei Women's Rescue Foundation. She received a Ph.D. in Criminal Justice at the University of Illinois at Chicago. Her research interests include violence against women, human trafficking, and victim decision making.

Dr. Brian E. Crim is assistant professor of history at Lynchburg College. He received his Ph.D. in modern European history from Rutgers University in 2003. Between 2001 and 2005, Crim served as an intelligence analyst with the U.S. Department of Defense and Department of Homeland Security where he worked on Near Eastern affairs and right-wing extremism in Europe and the United States. Crim's primary areas of research include political violence and paramilitary politics in twentieth-century Europe. His recent publications include articles in the *Journal of Conflict Studies, Film and History,* and *The Journal of Interdisciplinary Jewish Studies.*

James B. Grassano is a fitness for duty coordinator at Babcock and Wilcox Nuclear Operations Group. Mr. Grassano, a former law enforcement officer in South Carolina, has received degrees from the University of South Carolina (BS) and (MCJ). His research interests include police policy and procedures, and the victimization of women and children. Other publications by Mr. Grassano may be found in *Corrections Compendium* and *Corrections Today.*

Dr. Sunita Manian is an associate professor of political economy and coordinator of the Interdisciplinary Studies Program at Georgia College and State University. Her area of research focuses on gender and economic development as it pertains to South Asia. Her research methodology uses axiomatic game-theory as well as qualitative research drawing from interviews with organized and unorganized workers in Kolkata (India) and Bangladeshi immigrants in London, UK. She has published articles on Muslim immigrants in the UK.

Dr. Sabita Manian is professor and chair of political science and international relations at Lynchburg College, VA. Her research interests and publications include gender security, China-Taiwan influence on the Caribbean, critical aspects of international relations theory, Israeli politics, and globalization and gender as well as pedagogical articles on linked courses for a learning community, and on teaching about gender in Japanese history.

Dr. William J. Mathias is a dean emeritus and Distinguished Professor of Criminal Justice Emeritus at the University of South Carolina. Dr. Mathias received his degrees from the University of Georgia (BBA), (MA), and (Ed.D). His research interests include police procedures, child abuse, and school safety. Dr. Mathias has served on several legislative committees in the state of South Carolina focused on children's rights and safety.

Dr. Kimberly A. McCabe is a professor of criminology and dean of the School of Humanities and Social Sciences at Lynchburg College in Lynchburg, Virginia. Dr. McCabe has received degrees from Virginia Tech (BA) and the University of South Carolina (MCJ) and (Ph.D.). Her most recent research interests include police policy, child abuse, victimization, and human trafficking. Her other books include *Child Abuse and Criminal Justice Responses* (Peter Lang, 2003), *School Violence, the Media, and Criminal Justice Responses* (Peter Lang, 2005), and *The Trafficking of Persons: National and International Responses* (Peter Lang, 2008).

Dr. Margaret Melrose is a reader in applied social science in the Department of Applied Social Studies and Institute of Applied Social Research at the University of Bedfordshire. She has published numerous books and journal articles. She has been a consultant to national children's charities and a guest editor of the international journal *Police Practice and Research* (Special Edition on the Criminal Exploitation of Women and Children). Her recent publications include "Out on the Streets and Out of Control? The New Prostitution Strategy and Drug Using Sex Workers" in Phoenix, J. (ed.) *Regulating Sex for Sale*, Bristol, The Policy Press (2009), and a coedited work (with J. Pearce), "What's Love Got to Do with It? Theorising Young People's Involvement in Prostitution," in *Youth and Policy Special Edition* (2010 forthcoming).

Nhatthien "Nathan" Q. Nguyen is a criminal justice student in the doctoral program at Sam Houston State University and a sergeant of police with the Houston Police Department. Nathan's current research interest is human trafficking, especially sex trafficking from Asia.

Dr. Henry Parada is associate professor at the School of Social Work at Ryerson University, Ontario, Canada. He has published in the area of child protection, institutional ethnography, and community social work and education in Latin America. He is presently carrying out national Institutional Ethnography of the Children's Protection Systems in the Dominican Republic.

Dr. David H. Richards is assistant professor of international relations at Lynchburg College, VA. He has a Ph. D. from American University. His research interests are in the area of the Caribbean especially U.S.-Caribbean relations. He served as a reviewer for the International Studies Association's compendium project on "Caribbean Foreign Policy." His coauthored work,"APSA Teaching and Learning Conference Track Summaries: Teaching Research Methods," was published in *PS: Political Science and Politics* in 2007.

Dr. T. A. Ryan is a Distinguished Professor of Criminal Justice Emeritus at the University of South Carolina. Dr. Ryan has received degrees from California State (BS) and (MS) and Stanford (Ph.D.). Her research interests include women in the criminal justice system, educational programs for inmates, and female offenders. Other publications by Dr. Ryan may be found in the *Prison Journal, Journal of Corrections Education*, and *Corrections Today*.

Stefan Schumann is a researcher at the Department of Criminal Law, Criminal Procedure Law and Criminology at the University of Graz (Austria), where he currently coordinates an EU-funded transnational research project on "Pre-trial Emergency Defence." He had worked previously as a researcher and lecturer for criminal, criminal procedure and European law at the Universities of Bayreuth (Germany) and Vienna (Austria), and had passed the German Judge and Bar Exam. His research focuses on crime, criminal procedures, and European law.

Dr. Arvind Verma has been a member in the Indian Police Service [IPS] for seventeen years. He has a degree in Engineering Mathematics from the Indian Institute of Technology, Kanpur, and his Ph.D. in Criminology from Simon Fraser University (Canada). He has served as the Managing Editor of *Police Practice and Research: An International Journal* and he has also been an advisor to the Bureau of Police Research and Development in India. His recent publications include a book, *The Indian Police: A Critical Review,* and other journal articles. He is currently on the faculty of the Department of Criminal Justice and has been the director of India Studies at Indiana University, Bloomington.